CONTENTS

Legal Frameworks in the Built Environment

THE BUILT ENVIRONMENT SERIES OF TEXTBOOKS (BEST)

Executive Editor:	Professor Tony Collier, Dean, Faculty of the Built Environment, University of Central England, Birmingham, UK
Co-ordinating Editor:	David Burns, Faculty of the Built Environment, University of Central England, Birmingham, UK
Assistant Editor:	Jean Bacon, Faculty of the Built Environment, University of Central England, Birmingham, UK

ADVISORY BOARD:

This series of textbooks responds to changes that are occurring throughout the construction industry and in higher and further education. It focuses on aspects of the curriculum that are common to all professions in the built environment. The principal aim of BEST is to provide texts that are relevant to more than one course and the texts therefore address areas of commonality in an original and innovative way. Learning aids in the texts such as chapter objectives, checklists, and workpieces will appeal to all students.

OTHER TITLES IN THE SERIES:

Design, Technology and the Development Process in the Built Environment
Management and Business Skills in the Built Environment
Collaborative Practice in the Built Environment
Creating Neighbourhoods and Places in the Built Environment

LEGAL FRAMEWORKS IN THE BUILT ENVIRONMENT

EDITED BY JEAN BADMAN AND LAURIE GRIMMETT

School of Estate Management,

Faculty of the Built Environment,

University of Central England, UK

E & FN SPON
An Imprint of Chapman & Hall

London · Weinheim · New York · Tokyo · Melbourne · Madras

Published by E & FN Spon, an imprint of Chapman & Hall,
2–6 Boundary Row, London SE1 8HN, UK

Chapman & Hall, 2–6 Boundary Row, London SE1 8HN, UK

Chapman & Hall GmbH, Pappelallee 3, 69469 Weinheim, Germany

Chapman & Hall USA, 115 Fifth Avenue, New York, NY 10003, USA

Chapman & Hall Japan, ITP-Japan, Kyowa Building, 3F, 2-2-1 Hirakawacho,
Chiyoda-ku, Tokyo 102, Japan

Chapman & Hall Australia, 102 Dodds Street, South Melbourne, Victoria 3205,
Australia

Chapman & Hall India, R. Seshadri, 32 Second Main Road, CIT East, Madras
600 035, India

First edition 1996

© 1996 E & FN Spon

Typeset in 11/14 Caslon by Saxon Graphics Ltd, Derby
Printed in Great Britain by the Alden Press, Osney Mead, Oxford

ISBN 0 419 21270 1

A catalogue record for this book is available from the British Library

Library of Congress Catalog Card Number: 96–67188

∞ Printed on permanent acid-free text paper, manufactured in accordance
with ANSI/NISO Z39.48-1992 and ANSI/NISO Z39.48-1984 (Permanence of
Paper).

CONTRIBUTORS

Jean Badman
Head of School of Estate
Management
Faculty of the Built Environment
University of Central England
Birmingham

Peter Barrett
Senior Lecturer
School of Estate Management
Faculty of the Built Environment
University of Central England
Birmingham

Laurie Grimmett
Principal Lecturer
School of Estate Management
Faculty of the Built Environment
University of Central England
Birmingham

Richard Jordan
Senior Lecturer
School of Estate Management
Faculty of the Built Environment
University of Central England
Birmingham

David Lynch
Member of the European research
staff of John Tomlinson, MEP for
Birmingham West

Jan Russell
Senior Lecturer
School of Estate Management
Faculty of the Built Environment
University of Central England
Birmingham

Helen Smitheman
Solicitor
Solihull College

Also, for her contribution to various chapters on legal frameworks in Europe:

Sofie Bosma
University of Amsterdam

INTRODUCTION

This text introduces students of the various built environment disciplines to the effects which law has on their studies and subsequent professional practice. Legal constraints have a significant influence on all practitioners within this field, and an understanding of legal principles is essential for students who intend to seek employment within the diverse range of professions involved in the development, design and management of the built environment.

In addition, this book seeks to provide an awareness of the role of the broad range of agencies, both public and private, who influence the application of legislation and public policy.

Within this text are three underlying themes:

- legal issues that restrict, influence, control and sometimes even encourage, the work of those professionals who shape our towns and cities;
- how the law is made and by whom, and who is able to influence the law-making process;
- the legal principles which particularly affect the role of built environment professionals.

The book has two major objectives: first, to provide an understanding of the principles of English law; second, to examine the role of the 'key players' involved in making and implementing the law and to focus on certain important areas which are of particular concern to built environment students.

The content is focused on the English legal system and its application in practice. However, the material will have some relevance and interest to readers in other countries whose legal systems were founded on English legal systems. Thus, students in Commonwealth countries will find parallels when they compare the operation of English law with their own processes. American students will find interesting contrasts, yet some similarities.

As you develop your understanding and knowledge through this book you will wish to consider drawing on other books in the series. *Design, Technology and the Development Process* demonstrates the wider social and political issues and their relationship to design. This is the context in which legislation impacts on the environment. *Creating Neighbourhoods and Places* covers the development of larger-scale areas. Knowledge and understanding of legislative frameworks are especially important in the implementation of major projects and provide the back-up, understanding and knowledge to implement neighbourhood or area planning. *Collaborative Practice* explains ways in which professionals work together, and *Management and Business Skills* gives guidance on skills that we all need.

The series as a whole provides a complementary set of books to enable young professionals in the twenty-first century to work together, using the specialist skills of their own area of work whilst having a breadth of understanding, knowledge and skill about the environment, to operate effectively on a range of tasks, including in multidisciplinary teams.

STRUCTURE

It is acknowledged that in a single 'level one' text it is not possible to provide an all-embracing account of the legal aspects of the built environment, but having laid the foundations it examines in some detail the legal provisions applicable to a wide variety of specialisms, and provides stimulation for the student to delve more deeply into specialist areas.

Thus, the structure is in two parts. Part One (The Framework) comprises Chapters 1–6, which concern the law makers, the administrators of the law, dispute resolution, the influence of government policies, and the growing importance of the European Union on the law.

Part Two (Elements Of The Law In Practice), in Chapters 7–10, examines in detail specific legal issues which apply to the changing needs of a modern urban society and the environment within which that society operates. Part Two examines contract, tort, land law and legal controls over the use and development of land.

All the authors have used the same format, and thus each chapter begins with its theme, objectives and an introduction and closes with a summary, checklist, references and further reading. Workpieces within each chapter are designed to encourage discussion on the application of the law. It is anticipated that the book will be particularly useful to individual students undertaking project work in cooperation with team members from other courses in the built environment field.

PART ONE
THE FRAMEWORK

CHAPTER 1 LEGAL PROFESSIONALS   This opening chapter is about the various legal personnel. It considers how the legal professions have evolved into the two branches that exist today and looks at the nature of work undertaken. The controls over the legal profession and how it has sought to respond to the changing needs of society are discussed and other legal personnel including legal executives, licensed conveyancers and judges are included. The legal aid system is introduced.

CHAPTER 2 LAW AND ITS ORIGINS What are the principal sources of law, and how are they applied in practice? It is clearly important for those working within the built environment to have a basic understanding of how our legal system operates. Statutory interpretation, judicial precedent and the hierarchy of the courts are all issues covered within this chapter.

CHAPTER 3 DISPUTE RESOLUTION Whilst many people are aware of the role played by the courts in deciding disputes, there are in fact many other ways of settling disputes. What types of case will be heard by the court systems and how are they dealt with? When will tribunals or arbitrations be more appropriate? Is a less formal procedure more appropriate, e.g. conciliations? This chapter seeks to consider the range of dispute-resolving agencies we have in this country.

CHAPTER 4 KEY PLAYERS AND THE LAW No single agency or individual makes 'the law'. It is a response to a wide variety of so-called key players, whether they be international, national or local. Once generated, the law elicits a response from government, *ad hoc* agencies, the business community and of course the public, which in turn influences our environment. Hence the policies and legal controls generated by these players are critical to the organization and function of society and its influence on the built environment. Topics include the role of central government and in particular how laws are passed, the quangos, next-step agencies, local government and the public and of the increasing role of the European Union.

CHAPTER 5 THE INFLUENCE OF THE EUROPEAN UNION ON THE BUILT ENVIRONMENT Since the mid 1980s, the British system of law and government has been part of a wider European system. Decisions made by the European Parliament directly influence both the built environment and those people working within it. This chapter examines the increasing role of Europe, explores the primary sources of European Union law, secondary legislation, and considers the powers and functions exercised by the executive, the legislative and the judiciary.

CHAPTER 6 POLICY AND PROCEDURES

Often the nature of legislative control will be a reflection of government policy and procedures. However, policy and practice adopted at both national and local level facilitate the operation of this control. This chapter seeks to consider the wide range of vehicles used to issue policy, including White Papers, circulars, rules, standards, planning policy guidance notes, and the views of the courts on such policy.

PART TWO ELEMENTS OF THE LAW IN PRACTICE

CHAPTER 7 PRIVATE LAW: CONTRACT
People make contracts every day of their lives, whether it involves the purchase of a new hi-fi or a visit to the hairdresser. The same basic rules apply to these transactions as to the highly complex contracts of the business community. Whatever our role in the environment, it is important to understand the basic framework of the law of contract. Topics include formation, vitiating factors and discharge and remedies.

CHAPTER 8 PRIVATE LAW: TORT
Within any society there will always be conflicting interests, and in order to strike a balance between these interests the law confers certain rights and obligations on individuals. The term 'tort' means a civil wrong, and this law has developed through judicial decisions. Within this chapter the torts of negligence, trespass and nuisance are considered and many of the leading cases are used by way of illustration.

CHAPTER 9 LAND AND LAND LAW
What is land? Does it include built structures? Can its use be restricted? Is anyone allowed to cross it? How is it acquired? This complex subject is introduced in this chapter with an examination of estates and interests, land registration and third party rights. The value of land and property is such that it is particularly important to clarify the legal issues that can arise due to many people having an estate or interest in the same piece of land.

CHAPTER 10 THE USE AND DEVELOPMENT OF LAND
This chapter examines particularly important aspects of the legal control of the use and development of land. It considers the protection afforded to tenants of property and the rights of their landlords, and also discusses the duties owed by owners of buildings to persons lawfully visiting the premises. Emphasis is then placed on town planning legislation, which obviously is a branch of law which will influence all the readers of this book in their future professional lives.

THE FRAMEWORK

LEGAL PROFESSIONALS

HELEN SMITHEMAN

Wherever you go throughout the world, control mechanisms exist which attempt to promote economic and social well-being without incurring environmental costs. The rights of the individual as well as the community at large need to be protected so that society is able to feel confident about its future. Whatever the legal system, there is a need for a variety of personnel to ensure its efficient operation, and these people require good education and training in order to cope with the complexities of a rapidly changing world. The roles of these legal personnel vary from country to country but the example of those operating within the English legal system will be discussed by way of illustration.

After reading this chapter you should be able to:

- identify the different types of legal personnel in the English legal system;

- describe the historical development of solicitors and barristers;

- understand the stages of education and training of legal personnel;

- explain the different business organizations of solicitors and barristers;

- comprehend the work carried out by legal personnel;

- demonstrate awareness of the use of the legal aid system.

3

INTRODUCTION

All those working within the built environment will have contact with lawyers at some point in their careers. It may be at an advisory or consulting stage, perhaps to advise on contract planning, or later if things go wrong and matters go to court.

But what is a lawyer? The term 'lawyer' is a misnomer. In the English legal system there is no such role. It is a generic term for the providers of legal services, who range from barristers, solicitors, legal executives and licensed conveyancers to unqualified personnel in Citizens Advice Bureaux or other advice centres. Under the provisions of the Courts and Legal Services Act 1990, the range is set to increase.

HISTORICAL EVOLUTION OF THE LEGAL PROFESSIONS

The provision of today's legal services has not evolved overnight but has taken hundreds of years to develop. By way of illustration, let us consider the key periods in this development in England and Wales.

Period	Description of courts
Anglo-Saxon pre 1066	No centralized system Local courts – county and 100 feudal courts – run by landlords Church courts
Norman post 1066	① The Kings Court – mixture of functions ② Separation of judicial function from the Kings Council
Between 12th century and 14th century	③ Centralized legal system ④ Three royal common-law courts based in London but also administering royal justice throughout the country
14th century	⑤ Other specialist courts: Court of Chancery – equitable matters Admiralty – maritime matters Court of Chivalry – court of honour Ecclesiastical courts – church law
19th century 1857	Ecclesiastical courts lost jurisdiction over probate and matrimonial cases
Judicature Acts 1873–75	Abolished old courts Established modern court hierarchy
20th century	Changes to system of criminal courts

Figure 1.1 Historical development of the courts.

In the thirteenth century there were several varieties of legal personnel. There were advocates who appeared in the **King's Court**. The lawyers were known as **pleaders** because they pleaded cases before the court. They were divided into **sergeants at law** – senior advocates who could appear in the **Court of Common Pleas**, which was one of the King's courts – and **barristers**, who were student advocates. **Attorneys** gave general advice and advocacy. Originally they were the agents of litigants, and were used to represent the litigant at court. Court proceedings were often held at some distance from the litigant's home and so the help of an attorney was desirable. These men became known at court and were then identified as court officials [1].

THIRTEENTH CENTURY

In the middle of the fourteenth century the **Inns of Court** were established. This was a voluntary association of the lawyers. They would meet litigants in the chambers or in public places, such as St Paul's Cathedral, to give advice [2].

FOURTEENTH CENTURY

In the sixteenth century the attorneys were excluded from the Inns. The barristers and sergeants tended to associate with courtiers and statesmen. This enhanced their social standing and meant they formed a prestigious elite. (This view of the status of barristers persists today.) Also in the sixteenth century the **solicitor** emerged. The name originated through the function of soliciting or persuading the court to move cases along. To begin with, solicitors were considered to be inferior to attorneys but their role as property advisers meant contact with and the respect of large land owners, and so their status increased. There were also **proctors** in the ecclesiastical and admiralty courts. In 1739, attorneys and solicitors founded the Society of Gentlemen Practitioners in the Courts of Law and Equity.

SIXTEENTH CENTURY

Under the sweeping legal reforms in the 1870s, solicitors, proctors and attorneys merged into the single profession of solicitors. Sergeants were abolished and the court advocate became known as a barrister.

NINETEENTH CENTURY

From this strange collection of roles there emerged the two branches of the legal profession that exist today. Lawyers are either barristers or solicitors. To the lay person the most immediate distinction between solicitors and barristers is the use of the wig and gown worn by the barrister. **Solicitors** are perceived as the office lawyers who are the first point of contact for the client. **Barristers** are the courtroom lawyers

THE MODERN POSITION

who act for clients passed on to them by solicitors. However, that picture is not completely accurate: there are many solicitors who are litigation lawyers and spend much of their time in court; equally there are barristers who advise and draft and rarely appear as advocates in court. There is also the view that the barrister is the specialist and the solicitor is the general practitioner. Again this does not represent an accurate picture of the whole profession. Many young barristers do a whole range of work before concentrating on specific areas. Many solicitors will deal with contentious work (court cases) or non-contentious work (such as conveyancing or commercial cases). There are also other providers of legal services. These include legal executives, licensed conveyancers and 'para-legals'.

WORKPIECE 1.1

THE LEGAL PROFESSIONS

Working either individually or in groups, produce a chronological chart to demonstrate the development of the legal professions in a country you know well.

LEGAL PROFESSIONS ACROSS THE WORLD

Whilst we have considered the current divisions that exist between the legal professions in England and Wales it is appropriate to reflect on the fact that across the world there are numerous distinctions between countries and terms for those practising the law. Elsewhere in Europe, the general term of 'lawyer' does not exist. In France the *avocat* and the *notaire* have similar roles to those of the barrister and solicitor.

EDUCATION AND TRAINING

Clearly the knowledge base required and the skills necessary for individuals to become members of the legal profession are extensive. So how does one become a member?

SOLICITORS

EDUCATION   Traditionally there are two routes of entry: the non-graduate route, which involved a longer period of training and examinations set by the Law Society, and the graduate route, which requires either a law degree including the six core subjects, or a non-law degree. The non-law graduate is required to take the Common Professional examination. This course lasts one year. Both routes lead to the Legal Practice course, which also lasts one year. The student may study this at the College of Law or at universities which offer the course. Unlike the old Law Society finals, which were very academic, the new course attempts to prepare the student for work in a solicitor's office. At present there are 7500 places.

TRAINING   Having passed the necessary examinations, the student must undertake two years as a trainee solicitor. This is the clinical stage of training and the trainee obtains the skills of managing an office, interviewing clients, writing letters, instructing counsel and handling client money. The period of training is supervised by the Law Society and the trainee must spend time in different departments. If the Law Society is not satisfied as to the quality of training then the period of training can be extended. The trainee receives a minimum salary, which since 1992 has been £10 100 per year in the provinces and £12 150 per year in London [3], although there have been moves to abolish this minimum salary. There are currently only 3874 training places, and many consider that if the minimum salaries were abolished firms would offer more training places. This would, however, limit entry to people who are self-supporting and therefore tend to restrict the range of background of people entering the profession.

ADMITTANCE   What happens once education and professional training are complete? The trainee solicitor is formally admitted as a solicitor and their admission certificate is signed by the **Master of the Rolls,** who is the head of the Civil Division of the Court of Appeal. All practising solicitors are required to maintain a practising certificate and carry professional liability insurance.

How does the education and training of a barrister differ from that of a solicitor?

BARRISTERS

WORKPIECE 1.2

SOLICITORS AND BARRISTERS
Compile a table showing the differences between solicitors and barristers.

EDUCATION   Those wishing to become barristers must obtain either a 2:1 honours law degree, or a non-law degree together with the Common Professional examination. The student must then undertake the Bar Finals course run by the Inns of Court School of Law (Council of Legal Education set up in 1852). The course consists of practice and procedure, and there are mock trials and advocacy exercises using television and audio visual aids. There are also lectures and seminars on practical aspects of the court system rather than the law itself [1].

All prospective barristers must join one of the Inns of Court. One of the requirements is that the candidates must dine at the Inn 24 times over two years, in order to involve the student in the traditions and values of the profession. There is criticism of some of the outlandish practices involved here. Helena Kennedy refers to the need to avoid the corner seat in the Hall. At the end of dinner, bread rolls would be thrown at the occupant amidst calls of 'up junior'. The student would have to stand on the table and call for permission to smoke from the Senior. She quickly learnt not to sit there! [4]

Currently the Council for Legal Education offers about 1200 students a college place at a fee of £5200. There are proposals to allow other institutions to run training programmes for the Bar in the near future. Eventually there may be a common training course for both solicitors and barristers, giving students a greater choice of which profession to enter. However, unless the 'costs' of education and training can be reduced it is difficult to imagine how many more people will be able to enter the Bar.

TRAINING   On successful completion of the course the student is called to the Bar. Notice of the intention to be called is advertised in all the Inns and the chance to challenge the call is given. There is a calling ceremony at the close of dinner. The student can then be called a barrister, but cannot practise without the practical training period. This is called **pupillage**. The pupil barrister must find someone willing to act as a **pupil master**. The period of training lasts for a year. In the first six months the pupil watches the pupil master at work and carries out simple tasks. This section is unpaid. During the second six months the pupil can accept instructions and be paid for the work.

EMPLOYMENT

Once qualified, what type of employment can solicitors and barristers take up?

SOLICITORS

The qualified solicitor can work in a wide range of employment, including private practice, industry, business, local and central government, teaching or Law Centres.

A **Law Centre** is a locally or centrally funded body set up to offer advice and representation to people where there is a lack of other sources of legal adviser either in physical terms (e.g. inner cities or large housing estates) or in terms of lack of expertise in particular legal areas such as housing, welfare, employment or immigration. Law Centres have sometimes been perceived as rather controversial. The people who staff them tend to be more radical and political, using their work to champion causes as well as helping individual clients with their problems. The greatest number of solicitors are, however, to be found in private practice.

PRIVATE PRACTICE The average provincial practice is owned by two, three or four partners and employs one assistant solicitor, one trainee, two legal executives and seven support staff. The usual line of progression is to complete the training contract and obtain employment as an **assistant solicitor.** After two to five years the assistant may be given clients but is paid a salary and does not participate in the management or ownership of the firm. The next stage is an **equity partnership.** Equity partners are required to put capital into the firm and hence have a share in any profits or losses made by the practice. Equity partners have unlimited liability: if the firm's assets run out the firm's creditors can sue the partners individually. There are 420 firms with more than 10 partners. These firms account for 5% of the profession and they employ 34% of partners, 56% of assistant solicitors, 43% of all fee earners and 40% of support staff. They employ 68 231 out of the 165 129 of people employed in the profession.

The high-street practitioner, who is the first port of call for the client, is usually a general practitioner who covers a range of work. Most solicitors tend to concentrate on either **contentious** (court) work or **non-contentious** (non-court) work.

The large firms meet the needs of big business and finance and their work might include the conveyancing of large office blocks, dealings with business disputes, company flotations, mergers, takeovers, tax, banking and insurance. There are medium-sized specialist firms who deal with shipping, entertainment, libel and copyright.

The average provincial firm deals with a range of legal matters consisting of conveyancing, wills and probate, matrimonial, crime, personal injury claims, commercial matters, civil litigation and consumer, employment and welfare cases. The solicitor deals with the preparatory stages of litigation cases in contentious matters and supervises non-contentious cases all the way through.

Solicitors operating outside private practice work in building societies, finance houses, insurance companies and property companies. In large companies they advise on legal matters, carry out conveyancing and litigation and act as company secretaries. In local government they perform similar functions for the elected council, and the chief executive of the local authority is often a solicitor.

Location	Percentage of firms	% of Population in area
North	43	53
South	31	33
London	26	14

①

Number of firms	Sole practitioners	10+ Partners
8524	3435	420

②

Rank	Firm	Fee earners	Partners	Equity	Assistant solicitors	Work
1	Clifford Chance	1404	237	229	890	Comm*
50	Sinclair Roche & Temperley	142	42	32	61	Mixed*
100	Nicholson Graham & Jones	75	34	14	30	Mixed*

③

* Banking, Securities, Corporate, Litigation, Property, Company, Taxation, Insolvency, Shipping, Aviation, European Law.

Figure 1.2 Information about solicitors: availability of legal services according to area. ① Zander. ② *Law Society Annual Report* 1994. ③ *The Lawyer* 1995 'Top 100 Firms'.

BARRISTERS

The majority of barristers work from **chambers**. In London, chambers are owned by the Inns of Court and are rented to sets of barristers at below market rent. There are 225 sets of chambers in London. Each set of barristers usually consists of between 12 and 20 members and each has a head of chambers who is usually a **Queen's Counsel** (QC). The members contribute to the running expenses, rent, heat, light, typists' salaries and the clerk's fees. The **clerk** is the office administrator, accountant, business manager and agent. All the work is channelled through the clerk, who negotiates the fees and distributes the work. Traditionally this was a very lucrative post as the clerk would take a percentage of the fees and in some cases earn more than the barristers he worked for. The clerk holds a position of great power, determining which briefs go to whom and even influencing the membership of the chambers. There have been recent moves to change this position. In 1994 there were 5374 barristers practising in London and 2719 in the provinces. Since 1990 barristers have been able to work independently outside the operation of chambers. What benefits is this likely to bring? Will it make barristers more accessible? Will it help reduce legal costs? Only time will tell.

When barristers start to practise they cover a range of work but, having gained experience, most barristers specialize in particular areas. Generally the work consists of advocacy and litigation. The paperwork requires **pleadings** (court documents) to be drafted in civil cases. The barrister may be asked to give written opinions on different legal points and to advise on the strength of cases. Chambers may concentrate on **common law**, which deals with matters such as crime, contract, personal injury and divorce. **Chancery** chambers concentrate on cases of trusts, wills, probate, bankruptcy, tax, partnership and company work. Most of this work is document-based and the barristers do not go into court very often. There are also specialist chambers in areas such as libel, planning, tax, local government, shipping, patents and commercial work.

MUMMERY REPORT After the Mummery report in 1990 there were changes to working practices of barristers. Previously convention required that the solicitor and client had to attend chambers for a 'conference with counsel' appointment, rather than the barrister going to the solicitor's office. It is now possible for the barrister to go to the solicitor although in practice the former arrangement usually applies. Barristers may now advertise their services and professional clients may have direct access to the barrister, but the ordinary client must still consult a solicitor first. There is some logic in this arrangement as barristers spend most of their time in court and it is therefore difficult to arrange convenient appointments for all clients. The chambers building is not usually designed with the client in mind and often the client may wish to discuss matters with the solicitor which are irrelevant for the barrister.

THE 'CAB RANK' RULE   The 'cab rank' rule states that practising barristers are bound to accept any brief to appear before the court in the field in which they profess to practise. Special circumstances such as a conflict of interest or possession of relevant and confidential information may justify the refusal to accept a particular brief. The reason for this rule is that under English law everyone is entitled to representation at court: if barristers were allowed to pick and choose their cases, some clients might be unable to find an advocate. In practice, there are ways and means of avoiding unwanted work!

WORKPIECE 1.3

THE WORK OF SOLICITORS AND BARRISTERS

Decide whether the statements below are correct or inaccurate.

1. The average practice is between 10 and 20 partners.
2. The line of progression is assistant solicitor, equity partner and, finally, salaried partner.
3. There are 420 firms with more than 10 partners.
4. Small firms deal with company flotations, mergers, takeovers, banking and insurance.
5. Barristers work from Inns of Court which are owned by the sets of chambers.
6. There are 225 sets of chambers in London.
7. Barristers' work is negotiated through the court clerk in chambers.
8. Since 1990 barristers have been able to work independently of chambers.
9. Barristers' work consists of advocacy and litigation.
10. Common-law chambers deal with trusts, wills and probates.
11. Chancery chambers deal with crime, contract and personal injury.
12. The Mummery Report relaxed restrictions on working practices and allowed barristers to go to solicitors' offices.
13. The 'cab rank' rule requires barristers to accept any brief which they are free to conduct.
14. The rule allows for everyone to be represented at court.

CONTROL

It is important that all professions are monitored effectively to ensure that they conform to written rules and succeed in maintaining high standards. The legal profession is controlled by the Law Society, Inns of Court and the Bar Council.

THE LAW SOCIETY

The controlling body of solicitors is the Law Society, which was set up by Royal Charter in 1831; by 1860 the Society was setting an entrance examination for its members. Under the Judicature Act 1873 they enrolled solicitors of the Supreme Court. The Law Society:

- controls solicitors' education, admission and right to practise;
- maintains control of the keeping of accounts, handling of clients' money and auditing of accounts and receives accountants reports from solicitors;
- will take over a firm where the solicitors are incompetent;
- can strike members off the Roll if the rules of professional conduct are broken;
- runs the Colleges of Law;
- has club facilities in Chancery Lane, London.

The Council of the Law Society consists of 56 solicitors elected by members and 14 elected by the Council. There are 121 autonomous local law societies. Discipline is enforced through the Solicitors' Disciplinary Tribunal.

All barristers must belong to one of the four Inns of Court in London. These are Lincoln's, Gray's, Inner Temple and Middle Temple. The Inns have control over the admission of students and the call of barristers. Their function is to maintain the standards, honour and independence of the Bar; to promote, preserve and improve services and functions of the Bar; and to act for the Bar generally. The Inns of Court are run by **Benchers**, who are appointed by their fellow Benchers.

THE INNS OF COURT

THE SENATE   In 1960 the Senate of the Inns of Court and the Bar was set up. The Senate consists of 101 barristers, some of whom are appointed by the Benchers; some are leaders from the six circuits and the rest are elected by the barristers. This body supervises and makes policy. It is organized so that all four Inns can speak with one voice.

The General Council of the Bar of England and Wales (otherwise referred to as the Bar Council) was established in 1987 and its function is to govern the profession.

THE BAR COUNCIL

WORKPIECE I.4

WORD-SORT: CONTROL AND CHANGE

Decide which of the words below relate to either control of the professions, solicitors or barristers or changes to the system.

Inns of Court
Law Society
College of Law
Benches
Judicature Act 1873
Advertising
Court monopoly
Leader of the Circuit
1911 right of audience in County/Magistrates' court

Grays
Bar Council
Inner/Middle Temple
Chancery Lane
Senate
Established in 1987
Relaxed ban on advertising
Lincoln's
Eligibility to sit as recorders, 1971
Local law society
Right of audience, 1986
In High Court

CHANGES IN THE OPERATION OF THE LEGAL PROFESSION

As society's needs have changed, so it has been necessary for business and the professions to respond to those needs. The legal professions have experienced significant changes over recent years. What are these changes and how might they benefit society?

Solicitors are a profession and traditionally they have distanced themselves from any connection with 'trade'. Clients were expected to come to them and their professional integrity was above reproach. In recent years, things have changed and solicitors must now be business people as well as lawyers. This is reflected in the relaxation of the ban on advertising in December 1986. Prior to that there was widespread disapproval of such a proposal. It was felt that such activity would damage the relationship of trust between the solicitor and the client. Since then individual firms have marketed their services to varying degrees. One should consider whether this will result in cost comparisons being made by would-be clients and hence a cheaper service being provided.

Barristers have had a monopoly over court advocacy for a long time and have jealously guarded their domain. In fact in the seventeenth century an attorney was thrown out of court when he attempted to speak before the royal courts. In 1946 solicitors were given the right to appear in county and magistrates' courts. In 1919 the Law Society suggested that the two branches of the professions be fused but this view fell on stony ground. After the war, solicitors could sit as stipendiary magistrates. In 1971, solicitors became eligible to sit as recorders and circuit judges. They could conduct appeals to the Crown Court from magistrates' decisions. The next encroachment was in 1986 when solicitors could appear before the High Court and Court of Appeal in formal or unopposed hearings. There was a gradual recognition that the legal professions needed reform. There was an attempt to do this in the 1970s but no changes were made, due in part to the reluctance of the Lord Chancellor to implement any change. Lord Chancellors tended to be members of the English bar and as such held great loyalty to barristers. Prime Minister Thatcher appointed Lord Mackay of Clashfern as Lord Chancellor in 1989. He was a Scottish judge and, having no such loyalty, was willing to implement quite radical changes. These included the right of solicitors to qualify as higher court advocates and ultimately High Court judges. Despite great opposition by the Bar and the Bench, the proposals went through [5]. However, since then only a handful of solicitors have qualified to practise in the Crown and High courts.

WORKPIECE 1.5

CONTROLS

Using a country whose legal system is familiar to you, identify how the legal professions are controlled in order to ensure that they conform to rules and maintain high standards.

OTHER LEGAL PERSONNEL

These include legal executives, licensed conveyancers and judges.

LEGAL EXECUTIVES

Traditionally, legal executives were unqualified clerks who carried out much of the non-litigious work in solicitors' offices. By the 1960s there was a growing view that such people ought to be professionally recognized. Therefore in 1963 the Institute of Legal Executives was formed and this body is now responsible for the qualification of legal executives.

Legal executives can handle client work, manage branch offices and head departments. They may deal with the legal aspects of a property transaction, be involved in the preliminary stages of civil court actions, draft wills, draft company documents and advise on matrimonial or criminal matters.

LICENSED CONVEYANCERS

Once the conveyancing monopoly was removed, unqualified personnel who traditionally carried out conveyancing work wished to be able to operate independently from solicitors. A professional association which accredited such personnel was set up. Solicitors feared they would lose business to them but the qualification has not proved to be very popular.

THE JUDICIARY

A chapter on legal professions would not be complete without some mention of judges. Their role in the justice system is different from those referred to above, in that they do not provide a service to individual members of the public, but their function is integral to the decision making done through the courts.

At present only solicitors and barristers are promoted to sit as judges, although there is possible provision in the Courts and Legal Services Act 1990 for other legal personnel to become judges eventually.

The hierarchy of the judges is indicated in Figure 1.3.

Court	1995 Salary	Title	Number
House of Lords	£103,790	Lord of Appeal in Ordinary	11
Court of Appeal	£99,510	Lord Justice of Appeal	29
High Court	£65,912	High Court	98
Crown Court		High Court Judge Circuit Judges Recorder Assistant Recorders	98
County Court	£65,912	Circuit Judge	476
		District Judge	258

Figure 1.3 Information on judges.

The functions of a judge include:

● overseeing the conduct of court hearings (controlling the course of proceedings, keeping order and ruling on admissibility of evidence);
● determining disputed versions of facts;
● applying appropriate rules of law to factual situations;
● directing juries on evidence and the law;
● deciding on remedies or sanctions;
● dealing with matters on appeal.

In terms of the development of the legal system the most important function of judges is to interpret law, and perhaps to make it. Unlike Parliament, this cannot be done by individual choice: legal rules are made through the context of decision making in court cases. The most interesting aspect of this topic is the one of judicial creativity. Do judges make law and should they make law? A later chapter (on precedent and statutory interpretation) examines this issue further.

After the advent of the welfare state it was decided that public funding should be provided for legal services but, unlike the National Health Service, the scheme was always limited in terms of range and eligibility. Legal aid is given to people of low means to enable them to pursue contentious matters (Figure 1.4).

THE LEGAL AID SYSTEM

The system was established in 1945 and since then has gone through periods of expansion and contraction. In 1970 the first Law Centres were established, and until 1986 there was rapid expansion with the introduction of several new initiatives. In 1979 assistance by way of representation in the courts was created. The stand-by duty solicitor scheme was introduced in 1983 and there was an increase in criminal and divorce work. Not surprisingly, there was a huge increase in legal aid, from £8 million in 1969 to £265 million in 1986, which is clearly a drain on public funds.

The Legal Aid Act 1988 introduced drastic changes and by 1992 there was general recognition of a legal aid crisis.

Between 1945 and 1988 legal aid had been controlled by the Law Society, with money from the Treasury coming via the Lord Chancellor's department. The annual amount spent on legal aid continued to increase and in 1986 the government decided to scrutinize the scheme and proposed changes. Many of these changes were not implemented but one, the creation of the Legal Aid Board, was initiated. It was considered that the Law Society had too much of a vested interest in spending as much money as possible, and the Legal Aid Board was created to take over the Law Society's role [3].

When Lord Mackay was appointed he was determined to reform the legal aid system and in 1992 he indicated that the increases in legal aid had to cease. (By 1991 the cost was £900 million.) There were various ways of controlling legal aid, one of which was to reduce the number of people eligible for aid; another was to limit payments made to the lawyers. The second option was preferred because there was less public criticism of that course. However, the budget was so out of control that the Lord Chancellor imposed savage cuts in eligibility. The lawyers

Type	Covers	Eligibility		Granted By
		Means	Merits	
Green Form	Preliminary advice. No representation.	Disposable income limit £72 per week. Capital £1000.	No merits test	Assessed by solicitor at first interview
Assistance by way of representation	Civil representation in magistrates' court.	Disposable income limit £156 per week.	Merits test – are there reasonable grounds for taking the case?	Legal Aid Board
Civil Legal Aid Certificate	Representation in civil cases.	Lower income £2425 per annum Upper income £7187 per annum.	Merits test as above	Legal Aid Board
Duty Solicitor Scheme	Advice at police stations. Representation at court.	None	None	Legal Aid Board
Criminal Legal Aid Order	Representation in criminal courts.	Lower income limit £48 per week. Contributions above that figure.	Merits test S22 Legal Aid Act 1988	Magistrates' court

Figures applicable as from April 1995

Figure 1.4 Legal aid scheme.

fought against these cuts but were unsuccessful. There will have to be radical changes in the way legal services are provided if the legal system is to serve properly the needs of society.

Legal aid exists throughout Europe for people below a certain level of income.

THE SYSTEM OF LEGAL AID

At some time during your life you may be involved in a dispute that needs to be taken to litigation. Often individuals are frightened of the law, unsure of the system and worried by the possible costs. For those individuals below a certain level of income a system of legal aid often exists. Find out whether such a system exists and how it operates in the country where you are a student.

SUMMARY

The legal professions have always been subject to change. This is principally because society's requirements for its legal services change over time. The rate of change at the end of the twentieth century is now more rapid than at any time in the last 100 years. The legal professions must adapt themselves to current needs or else the legal advisory system will crumble and be of very limited value as far as legal services are concerned.

This chapter has:

- outlined the historical development of the legal professions;
- examined the qualifications and training of the various providers of legal services;
- considered the work carried out by the legal professionals and the environment within which they operate;
- described briefly recent changes to the legal professions;
- examined the operation of the legal aid system.

CHECKLIST

This chapter has considered:

- the use and development of different types of legal personnel from the Middle Ages to present-day solicitors and barristers;
- the division of legal professionals into two branches with separate education, training and work;
- the perception of barristers as advocates and solicitors as office lawyers;
- the recent changes to legal services which are blurring the distinction and opening up work to other personnel such as legal executives, licensed conveyancers and para-legals;
- access to justice through the legal aid system and its present crisis, which is limiting the amount of public money spent.

REFERENCES

1. Berlins, M. and Dyer, C. (1994) *The Law Machine*, Penguin, London.
2. Seldon, A. (1987) *Law and Lawyer in Perspective*, Penguin, London.

3.   Rozenburg, J. (1995) *The Search for Justice*, Hodder & Stoughton, London.
4.   Kennedy, H. (1993) *Eve Was Framed*, Vintage, London.
5.   Law Society Annual Report. *New Law Journal*, 2.12.94.

FURTHER READING

Bocker, M., Marzheuser, B., Nusser, M. and Scheja, K. (1992) *Germany: Practical Commercial Law*, Longman, London.

Cairns, W. and McKeon, R. (1995) *Introduction to French Law*, Cavendish, London.

Harris, P. (1993) *An Introduction to Law*, 4th edn, Butterworths, London.

McKie, S. (1993) *Legal Research: how to find and understand the Law*, Cavendish, London.

LAW – ITS ORIGIN AND OPERATION

RICHARD JORDAN

It is imperative that those who work within the built environment have a basic understanding of the way in which our legal system works. In order to be able to take prudent decisions and give effective advice, we need to be aware of the principal sources of law and the way in which the law is applied in practice. Put simply, the law comprises a body of principles, and this chapter will explain how these principles come into existence and the way in which they are applied by those who are responsible for administering justice.

After reading this chapter you should be able to:

* explain the two principal sources of law;

* understand what is meant by statutory interpretation and refer to the traditional 'rules' which are available to the judges;

* demonstrate an awareness of the way in which statutory interpretation 'works' in practice;

* understand what is meant by the hierarchy of the courts and the doctrine of judicial precedent;

* critically analyse the way in which precedent operates.

One of our most important constitutional doctrines is that of parliamentary sovereignty, otherwise known as the supremacy of parliament. This means that, because Parliament is democratically elected (in theory at least), and there is no written constitution regulating parliamentary power, there is no limit as to the law which it can make through the legislative process (Chapters 4 and 5).

Allied to the doctrine of parliamentary sovereignty is the doctrine of the separation of powers whereby the respective roles of Parliament and the judges are entirely distinct. Parliament's job is to make the law and to state clearly what the law is in an Act of Parliament. The judge's task is then to interpret the Act in order to find Parliament's intention and to apply the law in the subject case. Where the intention of Parliament is clear, then it must apply and there is no wherewithal within our constitution for a judge to 'overrule' Parliament. Whether this is appropriate is perhaps a matter for consideration.

When we say that law is made by Parliament through legislation, Parliament comprises the monarch, the House of Commons and the House of Lords. The role of the monarch stems from tradition and today is a mere formality. Historically, the monarch would play a far greater role in the legislative process, with the first real tranche of legislation emanating from the twelfth century in the reign of Henry II. At this time, it was normal for the monarch to make legislation, with the assistance of a selected group of nobles and clergy gathered from the shires. Today, however, the Queen will attend the new session of Parliament where she will read a statement prepared by the Prime Minister containing the government's proposals for the forthcoming session. Otherwise, apart from giving the Royal Assent to each new Act of Parliament (an essential provision but, again, a formality), the Queen plays no part in parliamentary proceedings.

Similarly, the role of the House of Lords in the legislative process has declined over the years. This House sits as the Upper House of the legislature and predominantly comprises hereditary peers and non-elected members. It has had its power reduced substantially by the Parliament Acts, 1911 and 1949, so that its role today is primarily one of scrutiny. For instance, the power of the House of Lords to veto new legislation has been repealed in favour of the power merely to delay proceedings by one year. However, it should not be thought that the House of Lords is without considerable influence. It is still highly regarded and, as a debating forum, continues to play a crucial role. Although the views of its members can in theory be disregarded by the House of Commons, this will seldom be the case and they will inevitably have an impact on the bulk of new legislation.

By far the most important parliamentary body today is the House of Commons, which currently comprises 651 democratically elected members. Included among these are the Prime Minister together with the majority of government ministers. In view of the effect of parliamentary sovereignty and the reduced power of the House of Lords, legislation is almost entirely a product of the majority party's policies. It is not the purpose of this chapter to examine in detail the procedure of passing legislation, which is dealt with in Chapter 4, but a brief outline will be of assistance.

One must consider how the component parts of Parliament inter-link in order to progress a 'Bill' to become an Act.

A draft Bill is prepared by civil servants on behalf of the government, after which a number of stages have to be completed prior to the passing of a new Act of Parliament.

- It undergoes the formality of a first reading in the House of Commons, where its title is read out by the Clerk of the House and Members are invited to inspect the draft.
- A second reading takes place in which the House debates the principles of its content.
- Each clause of the Bill is then examined in detail by a standing committee.
- The committee reports back to the House of Commons, which votes on any suggested amendments.
- The Bill is given a third reading in the House at which verbal alterations only are allowed.

After the Bill has passed the third reading, it is referred to the House of Lords for comment and sometimes proposals for amendment. When it has successfully passed through the Lords, it must finally receive the Royal Assent which, as previously mentioned, is now a formality and never refused. There may be as many as 80 Bills that become Acts going through this process during each parliamentary session (e.g. Channel Tunnel Act 1987).

DELEGATED LEGISLATION

Whilst the basic framework for legal control of the use of land and buildings is laid down in Acts of Parliament, it is normally impossible for all the necessary fine details to be incorporated into an Act. Parliament's time is more effectively spent drafting primary legislation, leaving the finer details of control to be included in what is known as delegated or subordinate legislation. The power to issue delegated legislation is given to an individual or specific body by the parent Act. The use of delegated legislation has particular advantages over Acts of Parliament in that it allows government ministers greater flexibility to respond to rapidly changing circumstances. There will not always be a requirement for delegated legislation to be laid before Parliament, and hence in such cases no formal parliamentary scrutiny of such proposals will be provided.

The main forms of delegated legislation are:

● statutory instruments, of which as many as 2500 may be made in any one year (compared with fewer than 80 Acts);

● by-laws, which are made by local authorities and other public bodies.

STATUTORY INSTRUMENTS (SIs)

These are documents prepared by government departments and published by Her Majesty's Stationery Office (HMSO). In view of the fact that the principles of law have already been established by Parliament, statutory instruments are generally subject to broader consultation or scrutiny during their preparation. Often regulations may be produced in draft to allow for comment before the final instrument is laid before Parliament for approval. This is merely a procedure to inform members, and there will not necessarily be an opportunity to debate the issues.

Is there any parliamentary control over statutory instruments? It would appear that control is limited, with many instruments which are likely to have little importance merely being 'laid before' Parliament for a period of time, usually 40 days, after which, if there has not been a resolution of Parliament to reject it (a 'negative resolution'), the instrument comes into force. Statutory instruments passed by the 'negative' process (i.e. they take effect if members do not challenge them) now account for the majority of cases.

However, there is also an 'affirmative' procedure, which requires a resolution of approval from both Houses. This procedure is normally, but not exclusively, used for regulations which may increase taxes or charges.

Since 1973, a parliamentary committee (the Joint Select Committee on Statutory Instruments) has existed to review statutory instruments from a technical point of view – for example, to ensure that they conform to a satisfactory administrative standard. Although it is not the purpose of the committee to consider policy issues, it does consider every statutory instrument produced and hence items of concern may be brought before Parliament. The committee is therefore a useful monitor of the SI process.

Given the concerns over delegated legislation in the form of statutory instruments, are there any benefits arising from this type of measure? They are normally quicker to produce and shorter in context than an Act. They can be amended to respond to change whilst still being within the spirit of the Act. Nevertheless, there is increasing concern about the use of delegated legislation and the lack of scrutiny available, particularly as delegation is increasing in areas of policy as well as the technical implementation of Acts. A report by the Hansard Society in 1992 on the legislative process (*Making the Law*) commented: 'We consider the whole of the approach of Parliament to delegated legislation to be highly unsatisfactory. The House of Commons in particular should give its procedures for scrutiny of statutory instruments a thorough review.'

The Hansard report also commented on the need for ministers to take into account more fully any comments and recommendations of the Joint Select Committee on Statutory Instruments – it is pointless debating an affirmative resolution without giving the Joint Select Committee an opportunity to report, as this effectively nullifies its role. Statutory instruments can be in the form of 'Orders' or regulations and cover a vast number of issues. Examples relevant to the built environment would include Town and Country Planning (Assessment of Environment and Effects) Regulations 1995. A particularly important statutory instrument relates to building regulations.

Since the Public Health Act of 1875, controls have been in force to ensure that any construction of buildings is undertaken to particular standards. Whilst in the early days local authorities exercised these controls through by-laws, in more recent years legislation has delegated power to establish regulations which will ensure consistency across the country. Current legislation is the 1984 Building Act, which empowered the Secretary of State to make Building Regulations, the most recent of which were issued in 1991. The regulations apply to any 'building work' or 'material' change of use of a building and as such it is quite common for building regulations approval to be required from a local authority even in cases where planning permission is not required (e.g. permitted development under the General Permitted Development Order). Normally local authority building control officers will inspect such work but the Secretary of State may designate others as approved inspectors (to date only one other approved inspector has been designated).

Local authorities lay down set procedures for the approval of work, and contravention of the Building Regulations can render a person, on summary conviction in the magistrates' court, liable to a fine. Work may be pulled down by the local authority but it is more likely that the owner will be recommended to make necessary remedial works or pull down the structure themselves.

BUILDING REGULATIONS

WORKPIECE 2.1

PARLIAMENTARY SOVEREIGNTY

What justification is there for decreasing the legislative power of the House of Lords?

What is meant by 'parliamentary sovereignty' and what effect does this have upon the role of the courts?

The delegation of a law-making power to a Ministry of the Crown usually results in secondary legislation known as a statutory instrument. When the power is delegated to a corporate body such as a local authority, nationalized industry or privatized utility the resulting legislation is known as a by-law.

BY-LAWS

Historically the term 'by-law' would mean a 'town law' and is possibly of Scandinavian origin. More recently, with the extension to transport undertakings and utilities, the term 'by' is used in its ordinary sense meaning secondary or incidental. All by-laws must be signed by a Minister of the Crown. In the case of local authority by-laws, the seal of the council is required followed by approval by the Secretary of State for the Environment. There is also a need for the documents to be published.

By-laws should be reasonable and must be consistent with the law in general; they should also be certain (i.e. not ambiguous). The Department of the Environment publishes 'model by-laws' in an attempt to provide suitable guidance. Examples of by-laws might include the requirement that dogs should not be allowed to foul footpaths, that no ball games should be played, or others for 'the good rule of government of a district and the suppression or prevention of nuisances'.

STATUTORY INTERPRETATION

As mentioned above, under the doctrine of the separation of powers, it is Parliament's job to make the law and the judges' job to interpret and apply the law in each given set of circumstances. Whilst this latter role would appear to be straightforward in theory, the vast amount of case law on the subject demonstrates that this is certainly not the case. At the time an Act of Parliament is drafted, it is virtually impossible for the draftsman to foresee all those future sets of circumstances to which the law will apply. Consequently, occasions arise where the meaning of the Act is called into question and often has to be decided by the judges. In order to decide upon the meaning of the particular document, the courts have developed certain 'rules' of interpretation. What are these rules and how have they been utilized by the courts? The four primary ones are the literal rule, the golden rule, the mischief rule and the ejusdem generis rule.

THE LITERAL RULE   This rule is favoured by the most traditional judges and requires that the ordinary grammatical meaning of the words is taken and applied in each case. Even where such application results in an absurd decision or one which could quite simply be deemed 'wrong', the traditionalist argument is that this is no concern for the judiciary but a matter for Parliament. If a gap or flaw is found in the Act in question, it cannot be filled or rectified by the judges but must be subject to amending legislation. Such a belief is demonstrated by the words of Lord Simonds in *Magor and St Mellons RDC* v. *Newport Corporation* (1951) [1]:

> ... the power and duty of the court to travel outside them [the words of the statute] on a voyage of discovery are strictly limited ... If a gap is disclosed, the remedy lies in an amending Act.'

The operation of the rule, together with an example of its shortcomings, can be demonstrated by looking at the well-known case of *Fisher* v. *Bell* [2].

A shopkeeper was prosecuted under the Restriction of Offensive Weapons Act 1959 for displaying a flick knife in his shop window. Behind the knife was a ticket with the words 'Ejector knife – 4s'. It was alleged that he was in contravention of the Act which made it an offence for a person to offer such an item for sale. The shopkeeper was acquitted. In contract law, the display of an item in a shop window constitutes an invitation to treat as opposed to an offer for sale.

This case illustrates the problems associated with the literal rule. Arguably, the purpose of the Act was to prohibit such occurrences as the display of such items in shops and it is not unreasonable, therefore, to suggest that the decision was, in one sense at least, wrong. There are many examples of the way in which the literal rule can lead to seemingly absurd decisions. One relatively recent case which relates to the built environment is that of *Cresswell* v. *BOC Ltd* (1980) [3].

Here, rating exemption was sought on the basis that the applicant's fish farm fell within the statutory provisions governing agricultural buildings and land. The essential question for the court was whether or not 'fish' came within the definition of 'livestock'. The Court of Appeal, in applying the literal rule, held that they were not. Consequently, fish farms were expressly afforded rating exemption in the Local Government, Planning and Land Act 1980.

THE GOLDEN RULE The golden rule is really an extension of the literal rule. Where the application of the ordinary grammatical meaning of the words used would lead to an absurdity, or there is more than one possible meaning of the words used, the judge is able to interpret the words by having regard to the statute as a whole in order to give effect to Parliament's intention.

The case of *Re Sigsworth* (1935) [4] is often cited as an example of the use of the golden rule. It concerned the interpretation of the Administration of Estates Act 1925 in circumstances where a son had murdered his mother. The mother had died without having made a will and the Act provided for the property of an intestate to be distributed amongst the next of kin. A pure application of the literal rule would have conferred such a benefit on the son but the court held otherwise on the basis that it is a general underlying principle of law that a person ought not to benefit from his own wrong.

THE MISCHIEF RULE This rule allows the judge to interpret a statute by asking what 'mischief' it was designed to prevent. It is otherwise often referred to as the rule in *Heydon's* case (1584) [5] in which the court asked the following questions:

● What was the common law before the making of the Act?
● What was the mischief and defect for which the common law did not provide?
● What remedy hath Parliament resolved and appointed to cure the disease of the commonwealth?
● What is the true reason for the remedy?

The mischief rule is favoured by those within the judiciary who advocate the purposive approach and strive to unearth Parliament's intention regardless of the actual words used. A good example of the rule in operation can be found in *Gardiner* v. *Sevenoaks RDC* (1950) [6] which concerned the meaning of the Celluloid and Cinematograph Film Act 1922. Notice was served under the provisions of the Act on an occupier of a cave in which film was stored. The notice, which required that the requisite safety regulations be complied with, referred to the cave as 'premises'. Gardiner appealed against the notice, claiming that the cave did not come within the meaning of the word. The court held that the

Act had been passed for safety reasons and was designed to protect persons working in such an environment as this. Although it was not possible to say that all caves would necessarily constitute 'premises', under the mischief rule this particular cave was 'premises' for the purpose of the Act in question.

THE EJUSDEM GENERIS RULE   Literally meaning 'things of the same kind', this rule applies where specific words within a statute are followed by general words and requires that the general words are interpreted in the same context as the specific words. The case of *Powell* v. *Kempton Park Race Course* [7] clearly demonstrates the use of this rule. The case concerned the provisions of the Betting Act 1853. Section 1 of the Act prohibited 'the use of any house, office, room or other place ... for betting and gambling'. Powell was prosecuted for taking bets outside on the course but was acquitted by the House of Lords which held that the general words 'other place' had to be read in conjunction with the specific words 'house, office or room' and therefore related to enclosed premises.

It should also be noted that where an Act refers to specific words only, and these are not followed by general words, the Act applies only to those specific words and no others can be implied. In *Shepherd and Shepherd* v. *Lancashire CC* [8] the provisions of the Land Compensation Act 1973, Part 1, were considered.

The Act provides for compensation to be payable to those occupants whose properties have depreciated in value as a result of specified 'physical factors' relating to the use of new public works. These are specified in the Act as being 'noise, smell, smoke, fumes, vibration and artificial lighting'. In *Shepherd*, the claimant's property had undoubtedly depreciated in value as a result of the use of a recently constructed tip which had substantially affected the view from the rear of the property.

However, it could not be established that such depreciation was due to any of the physical factors contained within the Act. This was really due to the fall in amenity value and personal inconvenience, which was not covered by the Act and could not therefore be implied.

WORKPIECE 2.2

THE LITERAL, GOLDEN AND MISCHIEF RULES

Why is the adoption of the literal rule deemed so important according to constitutional theory?

What are the advantages of using the golden rule and mischief rule?

OTHER AIDS TO INTERPRETATION

Apart from the traditional 'rules' referred to above, there are various other sources available to the judge in facilitating interpretation. Amongst these are the long title of the statute, the preamble, the headings prefixed to a part of the Act and the schedules. However, one particular source of information to which judges have only recently been entitled to refer is *Hansard*, the reports of parliamentary proceedings.

As a result of the House of Lords' decision in *Pepper* v. *Hart* (1993) [9] *Hansard* may be consulted by a judge where the meaning of the words used within a statute is ambiguous or obscure, or where the application of the literal rule would be likely to lead to an absurd result, and where a clear statement made by the relevant minister in Parliament would resolve the issue.

Whilst the above rules have been presented as separate canons of interpretation, it would probably be more realistic to talk about two distinct approaches: the literal approach and the purposive approach. The advantage of the literal approach is that it promotes certainty, but it has been widely condemned in recent times in favour of the purposive approach, which allows a greater degree of flexibility to those seeking to find the intention behind the words used. Professor Glanville Williams has described the literal rule as:

> ... a rule against using intelligence in understanding language. Anyone who in ordinary life interpreted words literally, being indifferent to what the speaker or writer meant, would be regarded as a pedant, a mischief maker or an idiot.

Preference for either is derived from the judge's own jurisprudential belief. The former approach is preferred by the traditionalists, but the latter approach certainly appears to be courting favour in recent times. The planning law case of *Griffiths* v. *Secretary of State for the Environment* (1983) [10] illustrates the way in which a decision will often depend on the approach favoured by individual judges.

Mr Griffiths wished to develop his land and applied for planning permission accordingly. The application was turned down by the Secretary of State. Any appeal to the courts against the Secretary of State's decision had to be made within six weeks from the date on which 'action is taken' by the Secretary of State. The House of Lords held (by a majority) that 'action was taken' when the decision letter was stamped by a clerk in the office. Despite the fact that the letter was never posted and Mr Griffiths failed to receive notification of the decision, that date was final and he lost the right to appeal.

Lord Scarman, however, dissented, saying that it was unjust that the right to appeal should be lost in such circumstances: 'I would not hold that Parliament intended anything so arbitrary.' The remainder of the House, despite acknowledging that the result was regrettable, refused to fill the gap and took the literal approach to the wording used. Whether such a decision can be justified depends upon the importance attached to constitutional theory. Is it defensible for the judges to 'fill the gap' left by the legislature in the name of justice? Another good example is provided by the case of *Magor and St Mellons* v. *Newport Corporation* (1950) [11].

In this case, Newport Corporation expanded its boundaries by taking in a substantial part of two neighbouring districts. The parts taken were those in which residents paid the highest rates. Under the Local Government Act 1933, the two district councils were entitled to compensation from the authority which had benefited. However, the Minister made an Order amalgamating the two district councils. Newport Corporation argued that the new council was not entitled to compensation as the statute only provided for compensation to be paid to a surviving council. The two previous councils had been abolished. In the Court of Appeal, Lord Denning said:

> I have no patience with an ultra-legalistic interpretation which would deprive [the appellants] of their rights ... we sit here to find out the intention of Parliament and of Ministers and carry it out, and we do this better by filling in the gaps and making sense of the enactment.

Lord Simonds disagreed with the approach taken by Lord Denning. He stated that it 'cannot by any means be supported. The duty of the court is to interpret the words which the legislature has used.'

He then continued:

> It appears to me to be a naked usurpation of the legislative function under the disguise of interpretation. And it is the less justifiable when it is guesswork with what material the legislature would, if it had discovered the gap, have filled it in. If a gap is disclosed, the remedy lies in an amending Act.

The majority agreed with Lord Simonds and the councils lost their claim for compensation.

WORKPIECE 2.3

INTERPRETATION

What does Lord Simmonds mean by 'a naked usurpation of the legislative function under the disguise of interpretation'?

CASE LAW AND THE DOCTRINE OF JUDICIAL PRECEDENT

The other principal source of law is case law, which is sometimes referred to as common law. Many areas of law will be largely unaffected by legislation and will have evolved through time from the decisions of judges who have had to lay down legal principles in deciding the outcome in cases before them. It is a particular feature of case law that it is subject to the doctrine of judicial precedent, or *stare decisis*, which means that judges will have regard to those decisions in previous cases involving similar facts and, in certain circumstances, will be bound to follow them.

The significance of a precedent in any particular case is determined by the status of the court in which the decision was made. The doctrine of judicial precedent is consequently subject to the hierarchy of the court structure. In simple terms, this means that decisions arrived at in higher courts will be binding on those courts below, in cases where the material facts are sufficiently similar. It is therefore important to be aware of where different courts side within the hierarchy.

EUROPEAN COMPARISONS

In other parts of Europe, law is based on a written constitution and thus found in enacted statutes and decrees, the civil, criminal, penal and other codes, rather than made by the courts as in England, Scotland and Wales. There is also a strict division of courts through separate systems of public and private law (administrative v. judiciary), for example, in France and the Netherlands. Whilst judge-made law has developed in the administrative courts, there is much less discretionary power there than in courts in England and Wales.

HIERARCHY OF THE COURTS
THE HOUSE OF LORDS

As the supreme appeal court, the decisions of the House of Lords are binding on all lower courts. As a result of the judgment in *London Tramways* v. *London County Council* (1898) [12] its previous decisions were binding on itself. In 1966, however, the Lord Chancellor issued a Practice Statement which read as follows:

Their Lordships regard the use of precedent as an indispensable foundation upon which to decide what is the law and its application to individual cases. It provides at least some degree of certainty upon which individuals can rely in the conduct of their affairs, as well as a basis for orderly development of legal rules. Their Lordships nevertheless recognise that too rigid adherence to precedent may lead to injustice in a particular case and also unduly restrict the proper development of the law. They propose, therefore, to modify their present practice and, while treating former decisions of this House as normally binding, to depart from a previous decision when it appears right to do so.

Despite the content of the above Statement, there are relatively few instances of the House departing from one of its own precedents, and it is apparent that this is a power that will only be used sparingly. It is of particular use where the law needs to be brought up to date due to a change in the social, economic and political climate since a previous decision.

For example, in *Herrington* v. *British Railways Board* (1972) [13] the House had to consider the extent to which an occupier owed a duty of care to a child trespasser in the light of its previous decision in *Addie* v. *Dumbreck* (1929) [14] that virtually no duty was owed at all. In Herrington, a young child had been able to wander on to a stretch of railway line by virtue of the fact that the fence bordering the line was in an extremely poor state of repair. The child was injured and a case was brought against British Railways Board as 'occupier' of the property. The House of Lords decided to overrule its previous decision and held that a duty of care was owed in the circumstances and that British Rail was liable. Professor Zander explains that the reason for the decision 'appears to have been a change in the climate of opinion as to the acceptable distribution of risks between occupiers and those injured on their premises'.

THE COURT OF APPEAL

Those decisions made within the Civil Division of the Court of Appeal are binding on all courts apart from the House of Lords. As a result of the decision in *Young* v. *Bristol Aeroplane Co.* (1944) [15] it is bound by its own previous decisions subject to the following exceptions:

- A previous decision cannot stand with a decision of the House of Lords.
- There are conflicting previous decisions of the Court of Appeal in which case the Court can decide which to follow.
- A previous decision has been given *per incuriam*. This means that the decision was given 'in ignorance or forgetfulness of some incon-

sistent statutory provision or of some authority binding on the court concerned'.

It should be noted at this stage that the Criminal Division of the Court of Appeal is not bound to the same extent as, invariably, personal liberty will be at stake and it is deemed appropriate that each case should be considered largely on its own merits. In *R. v. Spencer* (1985) [16] it was said that the Court was justified in refusing to follow precedent 'if a departure from authority is necessary in the interests of justice to an appellant'.

THE HIGH COURT

The decision of a single judge sitting as a trial judge hearing the case for the first time is not binding on other judges within the High Court although it will often be highly persuasive and will generally be followed. Decisions of a divisional court, where three judges sit as an appeal panel, are binding on judges of the same division sitting alone but not necessarily on future divisional courts hearing appeals.

THE COUNTY COURT/ CROWN COURT AND MAGISTRATES' COURT

As the doctrine of binding precedent relies inherently on a comprehensive and accurate system of law reporting, the fact that the decisions in these courts are seldom reported means that they are not binding on any other courts. (Further detail on the jurisdiction of the courts is given in Chapter 3.)

WORKPIECE 2.4

THE ROLE OF THE LORDS

Do you agree that the House of Lords should be able to depart from its previous decisions?

In what instances is the House of Lords most likely to use this power and why, in particular, did the House consider that it should depart from precedent in *Herrington* v. *BRB* (1973)?

DISTINGUISHING

Notwithstanding the above comments relating to the hierarchy of the courts and the way in which a court is bound to follow a previous decision, a judge always has the option of refusing to follow a precedent by 'distinguishing' the subject case from that in which the previous decison was made. This means that the judge will consider that the material facts in the instant case are sufficiently different from those in the previous case so that the case is distinguished and the precedent not binding. An example is provided in the following two cases which relate to damages for nervous shock in negligence.

In *Hambrook* v. *Stokes* (1926) [17] the plaintiff had entered a shop, leaving her two young children playing nearby. The defendants' lorry, which had been left at the top of a hill with the handbrake unsecured, rolled uncontrollably down the hill. As the plaintiff was leaving the shop she saw the lorry, heard a crash and feared for the safety of her children. The shock of the event resulted in her becoming seriously ill and she later died. Her estate was awarded damages in negligence by the court which provided that the defendant owed a duty of care in such circumstances as long as the plaintiff witnessed the event with her own unaided senses.

In *Bourhill* v. *Young* (1943) [18] the plaintiff was a pregnant woman who was on a tram when she heard an accident further along the road. The accident had been caused by the defendant motorcyclist, who died shortly afterwards. When the plaintiff arrived at the scene of the accident some minutes later, she saw blood on the road which caused her to suffer nervous shock as a result of which she lost her baby. The court refused her claim for damages. It held that no duty of care was owed in the circumstances. It distinguished the case from *Hambrook* v. *Stokes* in that the plaintiff had not witnessed the event at the time it occurred and was not therefore sufficiently proximate.

When dealing with the doctrine of precedent, it is important to realize that only a part of a decision is binding. This is known as the 'ratio decidendi', which means the reason for the decision and refers to the principle of law as it relates to the material facts of the case. In arriving at the decision, a judge will invariably discuss the relevant law and suggest what the outcome would have been in various hypothetical situations before arriving at the ratio. Everything contained within the judge's speech which is not part of the ratio decidendi is known as 'obiter dicta'. These are not binding in subsequent cases but can often be highly persuasive, especially where they emanate from the most senior judges in the higher appeal courts. The meaning and significance of these two phrases will be illustrated by looking at one of the most famous cases in English legal history. It is generally acknowledged as the starting point for the recognition of negligence as a separate tort and has certainly had a considerable impact on the built environment in recent times.

In *Donoghue* v. *Stevenson* (1932) [19], a friend of the appellant purchased a bottle of ginger beer from a retailer and gave it to her to drink. The bottles had been supplied by the manufacturers, who were the respondents in the case. The bottles were made of dark glass so that the

**RATIO DECIDENDI
AND OBITER DICTA**

contents could not be seen until they were poured into a glass. While consuming the drink, the appellant poured what appeared to be the remains of a decomposed snail from the bottle into her glass and, after having become ill as a result of the sight of the snail and the impurities in the drink, she sued the manufacturers in negligence. Despite the fact that there was no contract between the appellant and the manufacturer, the House of Lords held that a duty of care was owed by the manufacturers, that the duty had been breached and that the appellant was entitled to damages.

The ratio decidendi in the above case was that where a manufacturer supplies a product in such a way that intermediate examination was impossible, the manufacturer owes a duty to take reasonable care to prevent injury to the end consumer. However, in the course of arriving at this decision, Lord Atkin made a speech which, although not formally binding on judges in subsequent cases, was so persuasive and widely acknowledged that it later became law. Lord Atkin said:

> You must take reasonable care to avoid acts or omissions which you can reasonably foresee would be likely to injure your neighbour. Who, then, in law is my neighbour? The answer seems to be – persons who are so closely and directly affected by my act that I ought reasonably to have them in contemplation as being so affected when I am directing my mind to the acts or omissions which are called in question.

Although these words constituted part of the obiter dicta, the law evolved so that they later became recognized as forming a test of reasonable foresight applicable to the duty of care in negligence. It will be seen later in this book how such words came to have such an effect on the work of professionals within the built environment, particularly in relation to surveyors undertaking mortgage valuations.

WORKPIECE 2.5

RATIO DECIDENDI AND OBITER DICTA

Using a case of your choice, distinguish the ratio decidendi from the obiter dicta.

SUMMARY

It is important for those working within the built environment to understand what is meant by the rules of statutory interpretation and judicial precedent. In particular, contextual awareness is necessary if accurate advice is to be given as to how the law operates in practice. This chapter has sought to provide such an awareness by focusing on the way in which the judiciary applies the rules with reference to selected cases.

This chapter has:

- introduced the fundamental sources of law;
- explained the rules of statutory interpretation and their application in practice;
- discussed what is meant by judicial precedent and how case law develops accordingly.

1. *Magor and St Mellons RDC* v. *Newport Corporation* (1951) 2 All ER 839.
2. *Fisher* v. *Bell* (1961) 1 Queens Bench 394.
3. *Cresswell* v. *BOC Ltd* (1980) RA 213 (CA).
4. *Re Sigsworth* (1935) CH 89.
5. *Heydon's* (1584) Co. Rep 7a.
6. *Gardiner* v. *Sevenoaks RDC* (1950) 66 TLR 1091.
7. *Powell* v. *Kempton Park Race Course* (1899) AC 143.
8. *Shepherd and Shepherd* v. *Lancashire CC* (1977) P&CR 296.
9. *Pepper* v. *Hart* (1993) 1 ALL ER 42.
10. *Griffiths* v. *Secretary of State for the Environment* (1983) 2 WLR 172.
11. *Magor and St Mellons RDC* v. *Newport Corporation* (1951) 2 All ER 839.
12. *London Tramways* v. *London County Council* (1898) AC 375.
13. *Herrington* v. *British Railways Board* (1972) AC 877.
14. *Addie* v. *Dumbreck* (1929) AC 358.
15. *Young* v. *Bristol Aeroplane Co.* (1944) KB 718.
16. *R.* v. *Spencer* (1985) 1 All ER 673.
17. *Hambrook* v. *Stokes* (1926) 1 KB 121.
18. *Bourhill* v. *Young* (1943) AC 92.
19. *Donoghue* v. *Stevenson* (1932) AC 562.

Keenan, D. (1995) *Smith and Keenan's English Law*, Pitman.
Zander, M. (1994) *The Law-Making Process*, 4th edn, Butterworths.

CHAPTER THREE

DISPUTE RESOLUTION

HELEN SMITHEMAN

THEME

Everyone has heard of the courts. They are places used to decide disputes which people have with each other. Some people may know the names of the different courts and others may have some idea of the sort of cases dealt with in each court (Chapter 2). However, there are other ways of settling disputes. The aim of this chapter is to identify and explain the functions of the dispute-resolving agencies which we have in this country. You will learn that many disputes are adjudicated outside the court system. Discussion of the processes is included together with description of the legal aid system, without which many cases would not be able to be taken to court.

OBJECTIVES

After reading this chapter you should be able to:

● identify the different forms of dispute resolution;

● describe the historical development and current use of the court system;

● understand the role of and creation of tribunals;

● appreciate the use of arbitration.

INTRODUCTION

Two of the aims of a legal system are to give people rights so that they can order their affairs and to provide a forum for adjudication if those rights are infringed. There is little point in giving rights without an enforceable system of remedies.

Disputes may be resolved in a number of ways using various processes, some of which are more formal than others. These include informal procedures such as conciliation and the formal processes of adjudication through the courts, tribunals and arbitration.

It would not be true to say that all dispute resolving takes place in court or other formal settings. Disputes occur when people involved in some kind of relationship, personal or business, disagree as to some aspect of that relationship. In other words they have a grievance. What can they do to try to resolve it?

Initially one person may have a grievance against the other person. That grievance may be abandoned where the person considers it to be trivial and not worth pursuing. The person may feel unable to pursue the matter or may not realize that they may have legal recourse in respect of it.

The next stage is to communicate the grievance and to try to negotiate a settlement. This process is carried out between the parties without outside intervention. It usually involves compromise by making concessions to each other. Often the parties will not admit any liability.

If the parties cannot resolve their dispute they may agree to involve a third person in the process to try to reach a settlement. This is important where the parties need to maintain a continuing relationship. Conciliation is often used, for example, in matrimonial or employment situations. The conciliator helps the parties to reach their own settlement and does not act as an adjudicator. Also the Arbitration Conciliation Advisory Service (ACAS) is frequently brought in to resolve disputes between groups of workers and their employers.

The next stage is use of arbitration. Here it is clear that the parties cannot resolve their differences and need a third person to make the decision for them. Arbitration involves the appointing of an independent expert to act as the decision maker. The parties must agree to the appointment and are bound by the arbitrator's decision. It is particularly used in complex and technical commercial matters. When there is a contractual relationship between the parties the contract may well include an arbitration clause, which would require the dispute to be placed in the hands of an arbitrator. Arbitrations take place in private.

The alternative to arbitration is the use of adjudication. This is the formal process of dispute resolving, and the case is taken to a court or tri-

STAGES OF DISPUTE RESOLUTION

GRIEVANCE

NEGOTIATION

CONCILIATION OR MEDIATION

ARBITRATION

ADJUDICATION

bunal by one of the parties. The court or tribunal will deal with cases within its jurisdiction, which is determined by physical location and the monetary value, nature and seriousness of the dispute. The case is usually heard in public and the decision given in open court [1].

You will see that whilst dispute resolution can take many forms, adjudication is the most formal, where concession and compromise plays little part. Under the adversarial system that operates in this country there is little room for concession and compromise. The general advice given by most lawyers, and recently by Lord Woolf in his review of the civil process, is that wherever possible court action should be avoided and only used as an absolute last resort. Why should this be the case? Clearly it is likely to be more expensive to take court action and probably more time consuming.

It is important to recognize that the forms of dispute resolution are not independent and separate. During the course of the dispute many of the various forms of resolution may be employed and negotiation between the parties involved in a court case often continues right up to the door of the court room, or even to the judge's decision. Some models of adjudication have conciliation as part of the process to try to avoid the confrontational aspect of the adversarial process [2].

CHARACTERISTICS OF THE COURTS
CIVIL AND CRIMINAL ASPECTS

The adjudication system in this country is divided into two main parts. The forums will hear either civil cases or criminal cases. Obviously the most significant part for the built environment professional is the civil aspect. However, for the sake of completeness both aspects are briefly discussed as it is sometimes impossible to look at a situation and predetermine whether it is a civil matter or a criminal matter. It is the legal response to that situation which characterizes it. There is a certain amount of terminology which is appropriate for civil and criminal matters (Figure 3.1).

CLASSIFICATION OF THE COURTS

Having introduced the hierarchy of the courts in Chapter 1, it is now appropriate to consider why this is important, what types of cases will normally be heard in each of the courts and how these cases are dealt with. Unlike the other agencies the court system in this country consists of a hierarchy (Figures 3.2 to 3.6). For two reasons, this is important for the provision of an appeals structure. When the losing party wishes to challenge the decision of the court, it would be very difficult to have a consistent line of appeals without a court hierarchy. Secondly, the process of law making through case law requires a clear recognition of which courts carry more authority and weight. It is the decision of those courts which must be followed in later cases, thus creating binding legal rules in those areas of law.

Features	Criminal	Civil
Actions	By the State against the individual	Disputes between private individuals
Purpose	To maintain law and order	To provide compensation
Courts	Magistrates and crown	County and High
Parties	Prosecutor and defendant	Plaintiff and defendant
Standard of proof	Prove case beyond a reasonable doubt	Establish case on the balance of probabilities
Decision	Guilty – convicted Not guilty – acquitted	Defendant liable or not liable
Penalties	Sanctions – prison, fine, probation, community service	Remedies – damages, injunction, specific performance and rescission
Examples	Theft, murder, assault	Contract, tort, land law

Figure 3.1 Legal terminology.

Inferior	Superior
Local court	No geographical area
Financial limits	No financial limits
Cases not recorded	Proceedings recorded
Subject to supervision	
County and magistrates' courts	High and Crown Court Court of Appeal House of Lords

Figure 3.2 Types of classification of courts.

41

Original	First court to hear case (court of first instance)
Appellate	Reviews decision of original court or appellate court below
Supervisory	Reviews proceedings of lower courts and decisions of public bodies

Figure 3.3 Court reviews.

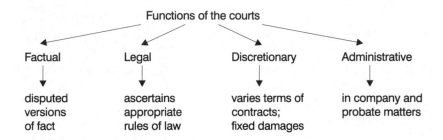

Figure 3.4 Functions of the courts.

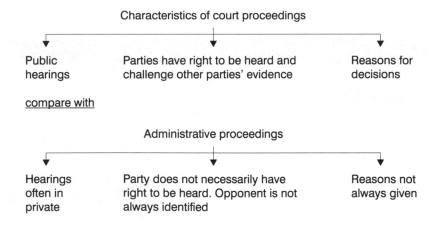

Figure 3.5 Characteristics of court proceedings compared with administrative proceedings.

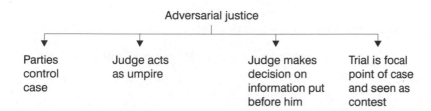

Figure 3.6 Adversarial justice.

The functions of the courts are divided into civil and criminal jurisdiction. Most of the courts deal with aspects of both, but the only court which has exclusively civil jurisdiction is the County Court.

The magistrates' court deals with a whole variety of different cases. It is most commonly thought of as the criminal court. All criminal matters start in the magistrates' court. The less serious cases (summary cases) are heard by the magistrates. The serious cases (indictable cases) begin in the magistrates' court but are transferred to the Crown Court for hearing.

On the civil side the court hears matrimonial cases, and also deals with civil debts such as council tax, charges for water, gas and electricity and television licences. As licensing justices they can grant, revoke and renew licences for liquor and gaming.

The Crown Court mainly deals with serious criminal cases. The Crown Court sitting in London is the famous Old Bailey. Matters are tried by a judge and jury. The jury decides on the guilt or innocence of the defendant; the judge oversees the conduct of the trial and determines the sentence if the defendant is found guilty.

The only civil jurisdiction of the Crown Court lies in appeals from licensing matters from the magistrates' court.

This court deals only with civil matters, but hears a whole variety of different cases. These include:

- contract and tort (subject to requirements of the Courts and Legal Services Act 1990 – see below);
- recovery of land – including trusts, mortgages, probate and dissolution of partnerships (value of these matters to be under £30 000);
- admiralty cases;
- company matters (value under £120 000);
- matrimonial and child disputes;

JURISDICTION OF THE COURTS

THE MAGISTRATES' COURT

THE CROWN COURT

THE COUNTY COURT

- race discrimination cases outside employment;
- sex discrimination in education or provision of goods and services.

Whilst County courts may deal with a wide variety of cases, they do actually work within certain limitations:

- geographical – cases heard within the defendant's locality or where the cause of action arose;
- remedies – the County Court is restricted in the remedies it can award;
- financial.

WORKPIECE 3.1

COURTS AND CASES

Find out the location of your nearest court. Identify what type of court it is and make a list of five different cases that have been heard over recent weeks, giving the decision in each case.

Before 1991, cases were divided between County and High Courts on the basis of value. Cases under £5000 were heard in the County Court and cases over £5000 were heard in the High court. Under the High Court and County Court Jurisdiction Order 1991, the position became far more complicated. The old financial dividing line was abolished and cases were determined on a number of different factors. There is now less emphasis on where the case is issued and more on where the case is tried.

The Lord Chancellor's aim was to achieve a closer match between the worth (substance, complexity and value) of what is at stake in proceedings and the level of judiciary, type of procedures and resources devoted to the conduct of those proceedings. In effect this means reducing the amount spent on court cases. This is of considerable importance given the fact that costs continue to rise.

The running costs of the civil system in 1994/95 were about £229 million and these are expected to rise by more than 75% over the next few years. Non-running costs are expected to show a similar increase.

As mentioned above the rules are quite complicated but, as a simple rule, cases under £25 000 are heard in the County Court and cases over £50 000 are heard in the High Court. Cases in between can be heard in either court.

In 1992, 3.5 million cases were started in the County Courts in this country. That was 5% down on 1991. Nine out of 10 claims were for money and the rest were mainly for recovery of residential property.

THE HIGH COURT OF JUSTICE

This court was created in 1873 under the Judicature Act and replaced a number of earlier unconnected courts. It sits in London and in 25 regional centres. The London court is found in the Royal Courts of Justice, in the Strand, a magnificent Gothic building opened by Queen Victoria in 1882. The cost of building the court came from money collected from people who had died without leaving a will [3], and 450 houses had to be demolished to make way for it.

At present there are three divisions of the High Court: Queen's Bench, Chancery and Family. A number of senior judges are involved in the High Court including the Lord Chancellor (president of the Chancery Division, but he does not sit to hear cases) and the Lord Chief Justice. The maximum number of High Court judges stands at 98.

THE QUEEN'S BENCH DIVISION (QBD)

This court deals with contract and tort cases as detailed above but only 1% of cases actually result in a trial. Between 1991 and 1992, the number of new cases fell by 25% and the number of judgments fell by one third, probably because more cases were heard in the County Courts.

There are two subsections of the QBD: the Commercial Court and the Admiralty Court. The Commercial Court sits in London, Manchester and Liverpool and has specially appointed judges to deal with banking, insurance and mercantile cases. This is an effective court with a substantial body of case law and a simpler court procedure. The Admiralty Court deals with shipping disputes – claims arising from collisions, defects in ships, ownership and possession of ships.

The Queen's Bench also contains a section of Official Referees. These are circuit judges who deal with technical and complex construction and accountancy disputes. Currently there are 63 Queen's Bench judges. The High Court also has appellate and supervisory jurisdiction through the Divisional Court.

THE CHANCERY DIVISION

The Chancery Division is a purely civil court and currently there are 17 Chancery judges. It took over the functions of the old court of Chancery and deals with matters of land, mortgages, trusts, probate, dissolution of partnerships and company cases. Its also hears tax appeals, insolvency and land registration appeals from the County Court and patents appeals. Most of the cases appear to be very dull but such cases command high legal fees by some of the most expert barristers.

THE FAMILY DIVISION

The Family Division hears matrimonial cases and also child cases, including legitimacy, maintenance and adoption. Under the Children Act 1989, cases are allocated to the most suitable court. This division of the High Court deals with the most important and difficult cases.

THE COURT OF APPEAL

The Court of Appeal hears appeals from the County, High and Crown Courts, and whilst the hearing is not a retrial the judges read the court documents and listen to counsels' arguments.

The Court of Appeal is divided into two divisions. These are the Civil Division and the Criminal Division. These courts can sit anywhere in the country but normally they sit in London. They have been known to sit elsewhere and in 1979, for example, the Criminal Division sat in Cardiff.

The Civil Division handled 800 appeals in 1992 and the then head of the Civil Division, Sir Thomas Bingham, considered that reform was needed to prevent more delays and backlog. This has been attempted by restricting the number of cases going on appeal.

The Criminal Division is headed by the Lord Chief Justice (Lord Taylor). He is probably best known as the judge who presided over the Hillsborough disaster inquiry, and subsequently produced the Taylor report on safety in soccer grounds. He represents a new breed of judge who, unlike his predecessors, has been willing to speak out in public about controversial matters. In 1991/92 there were 7000 applications for permission to appeal from the Crown Court. The court agreed to hear 2400 appeals.

THE HOUSE OF LORDS

This is the name given to the highest court in this country but is also the name of Parliament's second chamber. Parliament, or originally the King's Council, was the oldest common law court, although since the fifteenth century the judicial function has been carried out by the House of Lords alone. Up to 1844, both lay and legal peers could sit to hear cases and often the lay peers outvoted the professional judges, which did nothing for the quality of justice!

After that date, the Lord Chancellor and other peers who had held high judicial office could hear cases, but such people did not necessarily hold the best legal qualifications. The Appellate Jurisdiction Act 1876 provided for paid professional judges who were peers.

The operation of the House of Lords is different from the other courts. There are usually between nine and 11 law lords and often two come from the Scottish judiciary. Cases are heard in committee rooms at Westminster. The judges do not wear wigs and robes but are dressed in ordinary dark suits. The court room consists of a horseshoe-shaped table behind which sit the judges. The table is not raised on a platform as it is in other courts. The judges take a vote on a motion that the appeal be dismissed or allowed and the reasons for that vote are given in speeches rather than in a judgment.

This court has had a rather chequered career. In 1873 it was nearly abolished and today there are those who doubt the wisdom of a two-tier appeal system. The law lords are also criticized as being too conservative and 'pro-establishment'. This debate has been argued in Professor John Griffith's book *Politics of the Judiciary* [4], Simon Lee's *Judging Judges* [5] and David Pannick's *Judges* [6], amongst others. It is a fascinating debate and worth additional reading.

Today, the House of Lords has almost exclusively appellate jurisdiction. In 1992, for example, it had to deal with 67 appeals (44 from the Civil Division of the Court of Appeal and five from the Criminal Division; seven appeals from Scotland, six from the High court and five from Northern Ireland).

WORKPIECE 3.2

COURT HIERARCHY

Using the country of your choice, devise a chart indicating the courts in their hierarchy and identifying the types of cases heard by each court.

EUROPEAN COMPARISON

The structure of the courts in France, the Netherlands and most other European countries reflects the strict separation between public and private law. Hence a dual system of courts exists. In France, for example, private law cases will be dealt with by *juges de fond* with appeal to *Cour de Cassation* (which rules only on the correct application of law, not on the trial). Public law will be dealt with through administrative courts, then the administrative appeal court and finally the *Conseil d'Etat*. The *Conseil d'Etat* has the supreme and in fact dual role, looking at both consultative and contentious issues.

WORKPIECE 3.3

COURTS AND THEIR ROLES

Choose the appropriate answer for each of the following question.

1. Which is the highest court in England?
- magistrates' court
- High Court
- European Court of Justice
- House of Lords

2. Which court deals only with civil matters?
- County Court
- High Court
- Court of Appeal
- European Court of Justice

3. Which court has divisional courts?
- High Court
- Court of Appeal
- County Court
- magistrates' court

4. Which court deals with most cases?
- House of Lords
- Crown Court
- County Court
- magistrates' court

5. Where are summary offences tried?
- magistrates' court
- Crown Court
- Court of Appeal, Criminal Division
- House of Lords

6. Where are indictable offences tried?
- Court of Appeal, Criminal Division
- County Court
- magistrates' court
- Crown Court

7. Which of the following is an inferior court?
- House of Lords
- County Court
- High Court
- European Court of Justice

8. Which court deals with small claims arbitration?
- Court of Appeal
- High Court, Chancery Division
- High Court, Queen's Bench Division
- County Court

9. Which court is not part of the Supreme Court of Judicature?
- High Court
- House of Lords
- Court of Appeal, Criminal Division
- Court of Appeal, Civil Division

TRIBUNALS

DEVELOPMENT OF TRIBUNALS

The tribunal system has developed during the last 200 years and unlike the court system, which originated from the common law, tribunals are the creatures of statute. When Parliament decides to give new legal rights and duties through legislation there must also be provision for dispute resolving when it is necessary. Parliament could simply have filtered such cases through the courts, but it was felt for various reasons to be more appropriate to create a new agency in each situation. The courts would not have been able to cope with the influx of new disputes and generally the type of disputes required a more flexible and policy-orientated approach than the courts were able to adopt. The role of government has changed since the industrial revolution in the nineteenth century . Prior to that, the government maintained order, protected property and enforced contracts but did not otherwise involve itself in people's lives. However, since the mid nineteenth century, government has developed responsibility for the economic condition and social needs of the people. This did not happen overnight and reform of various aspects developed slowly, beginning with regulation of the workplace, the railways and, running into the twentieth century, the development of the welfare state. Today there are more than 50 different types of statutory tribunals dealing with specific issues, including the Lands Tribunal and the Rent Tribunal [2].

ORGANIZATION AND PROCEDURE

The organization and procedures of tribunals also developed in a piecemeal way. Unlike the courts where the processes have developed over a long period, with most courts now following the same types of procedures, tribunals tend to 'do their own thing'. Generally the procedures are simpler than in the courts, because applicants tend not to be legally represented and therefore must be able to follow the application. The process is not long and drawn out as in a court case, where there is a complicated procedure to follow before the dispute is actually heard in court. On the whole the nature of the procedure and the speedy resolution reflects this need for urgency.

The adjudicator comprises a panel of three people, of which the chairperson is usually a lawyer. Sometimes that is a statutory requirement and sometimes it is normally required as a matter of practice. Some posts are full-time (for example, the president of the Lands Tribunal) but others are part-time. The background of the lay members is related to the type of tribunal work. There is usually a 'representative panel'. For example, on the Rent Assessment Committee the panel will consist of a lawyer (who is chairman), a surveyor and a representative of the tenants. There is also a clerk to the tribunal whose role is to take notes of evidence and to give advice on points connected with the tribunal's functions. The clerk should not retire with the panel unless sent for to advise on a particular point. To this extent the clerk plays a similar role to that of the justices' clerk in the magistrates' court.

The formality of the procedure varies with the type of tribunal: some are as formal and adversarial as the courts and some consist of a more informal discussion round a table. The industrial tribunals are perceived to be legalistic and formal whereas the Social Security Appeals Tribunal adheres to an informal role. On the whole, hearings are in public except where the issues involve personal finance and matters of reputation, but reasons for decisions are not given unless requested and there is no duty on the panel to inform the applicants of that right.

Generally legal aid is not available for tribunal cases. This is a policy decision by government as to allow such legal aid would increase the legal aid expenditure enormously.

The appeals structure against tribunal decisions is not uniform. Sometimes there is a clear line of appeal (for example, in employment and social security matters) but often there is no right of appeal at all (for example, there is no appeal from the decision of the Vaccine Damage Tribunal). In such cases the only control is through an application for judicial review. The court will interfere only where there have been procedural irregularities.

EXAMINATION OF PARTICULAR TRIBUNALS

Statutory tribunals can be classified under several general headings: social administration, economic matters and revenue. Social administration includes personal welfare, pensions, educations, employment, National Health Service and immigration. Economic matters include agriculture, commerce, transport and housing. Revenue includes taxation, statutory levies, property, valuation and rating.

The tribunals which are relevant to the built environment include the Rent Tribunal, Leasehold Valuation Tribunal, Lands Tribunal, Local Valuation Court and London Building Act Tribunal of Appeal, Agricultural Land Tribunal, Arbitrators under the Agricultural Holdings Act 1948 and the Commons Commissioners.

There is general criticism of the way housing matters are divided between different bodies. If tenants think their rents are too high, their cases go before a rent officer and then the Rent Assessment Committee (or the committee sitting as a rent tribunal); if they wish to contest a notice to quit or get repairs done by the landlord, then the case is held in the County Court; and if the landlord attempts to get them out then there will be a criminal prosecution for harassment. Although this structure is confusing for many people, it was considered in the 1987 Civil Justice Review to be justified because the types of issues were sufficiently distinct to warrant separate treatment [1].

WORKPIECE 3.4

TRIBUNALS

Decide whether the following statements are true or false.

1. Administrative tribunals were established in the mid eighteenth century.
2. They developed because of the increase of government intervention in people's lives.
3. Social security tribunals are an example of a tribunal of enquiry.
4. The industrial tribunal deals with unfair dismissal, redundancy and other matters related to employment.
5. The Lands Tribunal deals with rent disputes.
6. Legal aid is not available for tribunals.
7. Members of the panel may be biased in favour of the government because they are employed by the department.
8. Tribunals tend to be quick, cheap and informal.
9. There is not a comprehensive adequate appeal system.
10. Tribunals automatically give reasons for their decisions.
11. Tribunals have the expertise that judges do not have to deal with the subject matter of the cases before them.
12. Witnesses must give evidence on oath.

ARBITRATION

The last type of formal dispute resolution can be found within the context of arbitration, which is used where the parties are in dispute but do not wish to take their case to court. Why should arbitration be the most appropriate course of action? There may be a number of reasons:

● They may wish to have the dispute resolved in private. Most court cases are open to the public; access is not restricted and of course matters may be publicized in the press.
● Using arbitration allows the parties choice of time and place as to the hearing. An arbitration could in fact be heard down at the local pub if the parties so wished! When taking a case to court the timing of the hearing lies with the court and dates given may be inconvenient.
● The parties may prefer arbitration as it is usually less expensive than a court case.
● The hearings tend to be matters of compromise, rather than the combative approach taken in court, and this will allow for a trading relationship to continue.

However, probably the main reason for choosing arbitration lies in the expertise of the arbitrator. Most arbitration disputes are technical or complex and most judges do not have the specialist knowledge to make decisions on these matters. This means that the parties have to instruct expert witnesses to inform the judge of the technical position, which is expensive and time consuming. Using the expert as the adjudicator shortcuts this necessity. The arbitrator should be someone with appropriate technical expertise, preferably experienced in arbitrations and also independent from both sides. Any one can be appointed as an arbitrator, though professional arbitrators are usually members of the Chartered Institute of Arbitrators. Clearly there must be a measure of agreement between the parties as they must agree on the choice of arbitrator.

THE POWERS OF THE ARBITRATOR

The arbitration should be conducted fairly in accordance with the rules of natural justice. The arbitrator can be given quite wide-ranging powers, including compelling witnesses to attend, directing the giving of evidence on oath and arranging for perjury proceedings if the witness lies on oath. These matter are agreed upon by the parties, who can also decide whether or not to be bound by the rules of evidence. Arbitrators' decisions are called awards and are enforceable as High Court judgments. They have discretion on whether or not to award costs and can also withhold their decisions until after their own fees have been paid.

TYPES OF ARBITRATION

Arbitration is usually referred to as commercial arbitration as it is used by people involved in a contractual situation. Bodies within trade association schemes (for example, travel agents) use arbitration. Contracts sometimes contain an arbitration clause stating that in the event of a dispute the matter should be referred to arbitration. This clause is binding and the losing party cannot resort to court action if they do not like the decision of the arbitrator.

Arbitration is also the descriptive term given to the pursuit of small claims (less than £1000) within the County Court. Small claims arbitration is a hybrid between the two. It is a formal type of dispute resolution in that a County Court summons is issued but such matters are separated from the ordinary County Court procedure. It was felt in 1970 that the normal process was unsuitable for small claims where the parties were encouraged to act for themselves.

The term 'arbitration' refers to the informal procedure adopted by the district judge who sits to hear the case. Under Section 6 of the Courts and Legal Services Act 1990 the court is to adopt an inquisitorial approach and assist unrepresented parties.

CRITICISMS OF THE ARBITRATION PROCEDURE

The decision-making process may lose safeguards incorporated into the court system, i.e. loss of protection of the rules of evidence and failure to rely on past cases, and the arbitrator may not have the same legal fact-finding and decision-making skills that a judge has. Although generally it is perceived that arbitration is quicker and cheaper than court proceedings, there may be occasions when a top arbitrator's fee is as high as that of a QC and there is a long waiting list for his time. There is also the view that when dealing with matters which affect the public it may not be in the public interest for the matters to be decided in private.

ARBITRATION

Decide whether the following statements are true or false.

1. Commercial arbitration is an alternative to court action.
2. If a contract contains an arbitration clause the parties can choose either option.
3. The party suffering the loss can choose the arbitrator.
4. The arbitrator should be impartial and an expert in the area of the dispute.
5. The Institute of Arbitrators has lists of professional arbitrators.
6. The arbitrator fixes the type of procedure used.
7. The award is enforceable as a High Court judgement.
8. The arbitrator has a discretion whether or not to enforce costs.
9. The privacy of arbitration is in the public interest.
10. It is commercially desirable that the procedure is convenient, quick and cheap.
11. Top arbitrators can be very expensive and there may be long waiting lists for their services.
12. Such cases are not appropriate for judicial judgment because judges do not have the necessary expert knowledge and valuable court time must be used to bring expert evidence to enlighten the judge.
13. Arbitrators do not necessarily have the right judicial qualities to make fair and just decisions.
14. Arbitration proceedings are more adversial than inquisitorial.
15. In claims under £1000 the plaintiff has the choice of arbitration or formal court action.
16. The Registrar deals with the arbitration.
17. The Registrar can make the judgment at the preliminary consideration.
18. Legal representation is encouraged.
19. Costs are not allowed.
20. The system has been criticized because courts and district judges are not consistent in their approach.

Arbitration is often used in France, Spain and Belgium to deal with disputes in specialized areas like contracting. Whilst there is a panel of independent legal experts who consider the dispute, their decision is not binding.

SUMMARY

Dispute resolution plays a large role in the legal system. This trend is likely to continue as activities are increasingly subject to regulation. However, traditional methods of resolution are being questioned and criticized. They are too expensive, slow and insufficiently specialist to meet the needs of the users, and consequently alternative methods of dispute resolution are currently being developed. There is constant talk of reforming the court system with the latest proposals coming from

Lord Woolf in his recent civil justice reform review. It will be interesting to see how the legal system will meet the needs of current society in competition with the growing alternatives.

This chapter has:

● identified the types of dispute resolution;
● examined the stages from grievance to formal resolution;
● looked at the different types of cases decided by the formal court system;
● considered the role of the tribunal structure;
● explored the use of arbitration.

WORKPIECE 3.6

DIFFERENT VEHICLES OF DISPUTE RESOLUTION

Compile a chart showing the differences between the courts, tribunals and arbitration under the following headings:

● Who uses it?
● Where is it held?
● Choice of agency

● Type of adjudicator
● Choice of procedure (formal/informal involvement of the adjudicator)
● Enforcement
● Adversarial/inquisitorial procedure
● Advantages/disadvantages.

CHECKLIST

● Stages of dispute resolution from informal negotiation to formal adjudication.
● Use and development of the courts in the Middle Ages, which comprised local, royal, ecclesiastical and other courts, to the modern unified system based on the division between civil and criminal; first instance and appeal courts.
● Changes brought about by the industrial revolution – increases in legislation and extended role of government leading to the need for tribunals as alternative forms for dispute resolution to the courts.
● Problems with litigation which makes the use of arbitration a more attractive option for many contractual disputes.

REFERENCES

1. White, R. (1991) *Administration of Justice*, Blackwell, London.
2. Jackson, R.M. (1977) *Machinery of Justice*, Cambridge University Press, Cambridge.
3. Rozenburg, J. (1995) *The Search for Justice*, Hodder & Stoughton, London.
4. Griffith, J. (1991) *Politics of the Judiciary*, 4th edn, Fontana Press, London.
5. Lee, S. (1989) *Judging Judges*, Faber, London.
6. Pannick, D. (1987) *Judges*, Oxford University Press, Oxford.

7.   Bailey, S.H. and Gunn, M.J. (1991) *Smith and Bailey on the English Legal System*, Sweet & Maxwell.

Abraham, H. (1986) *The Judicial Process, an introductory analysis of the courts of the United States, England and France*, 5th edn, Oxford University Press, Oxford.

Cairns, W. and McKeon, R. (1995) *Introduction to French Law*, Cavendish, London

Cairns, J.W. (1989) *Review of Legal History of Scotland*, Vol. 9, Legal Studies, 189–213.

KEY PLAYERS AND THE LAW

JEAN BADMAN

THEME

The influence of the law on the built environment is reflected in the way various 'key players' generate and respond to control and policy. These players may operate at different levels – international, national, regional or local – and every country of the world will have distinctive organizations to undertake these roles. This chapter seeks to consider a number of organizations in England and Wales and to examine how they are influenced in their function and operation within the built environment by other bodies and individuals.

OBJECTIVES

After reading this chapter you should be able to:

● identify the key players who generate and respond to control and policy in Britain;

● appreciate the various roles of such key players;

● demonstrate an awareness of how Acts of Parliaments evolve:

● be aware of the increasing influence of the European Union.

INTRODUCTION

In England and Wales over the last 20 years, changes that have taken place within government have been substantial, with reorganizations of central government departments and attempts to control spending and efficiency drives being a feature of the recent past. At local government level there has been a move to separate the responsibility for service provision and its delivery, to introduce competition between public and private sector (compulsory competitive tendering) and to enhance consumer choice – in short, an attempt to promote a more business-like structure capable of responding efficiently to the demands placed upon it. Policy to bring private sector practices into the public domain has seen a range of *ad hoc* agencies established both within and external to the government machinery. Quasi-autonomous non-governmental agencies (quangos), including agencies such as English Heritage and the Countryside Commission, have become more influential, as have those known as 'next-step' agencies (e.g. the Planning Inspectorate and the Land Registry) which were previously incorporated within government departments. Since 1972, with Britain's entry into Europe, the European Union (EU) has played an ever increasing role in determining policy and control over the environment. The European Commission, which is the executive for the EU, has used a range of legislative tools to direct policy within the member states (Chapter 5).

In a democratic society like the United Kingdom, opportunities exist through a variety of means to vote for a political party, at both national and local level, that advocates policies deemed important to us. As an individual or perhaps a member of a business organization, pressure group, charity or political interest group, we have a responsibility to contribute to the establishment and implementation of such policies.

Other countries outside the UK do not necessarily operate in a similar manner, though there have been major changes in the administrative and legislative control systems of many countries throughout the world in recent years. This is particularly noticeable in the old Eastern Bloc countries and more recently in parts of the African continent where state control and dictatorship have been the norm.

In the UK, parties that hope to gain political office must consider the opinions of the electorate, the financial support provided by the business community and the increasing window of opportunity and control mechanisms provided by the European Union.

No single agency or individual makes 'the law'. It is a response to a wide variety of so-called key players, whether they be international, national or local. Once generated, the law elicits a response from government, *ad hoc* agencies, the business community and of course the public, which in turn influences our environment. Hence the policies and legal controls generated by these players are critical to the organization and function of society and its influence on the built environment. By way of illustration, the structures of the civil service, quangos and next-step agencies are considered further in this chapter together with the various roles of central and local government, the public and the increasing role of the European Union.

THE KEY PLAYERS AND THEIR ROLES

CENTRAL GOVERNMENT

As society evolves, so its needs become ever more complex; it requires direction and controls, and it must be governed! How does this process take place?

At central level, government is concerned with three main areas of responsibility:

● the formulation of policy, which is made by the Cabinet;
● the legislative function of framing laws, which is carried out by Parliament;
● the executive function of the Civil Service, which advises ministers and organizes implementation of policy and enforcement.

In the day-to-day running of the policy planning system, 'the Cabinet may propose and the Houses of Parliament decide or legitimate new policy, but it is the Civil Service who administers' [1]. Decisions on government policy can thus be influenced by lobbying within any of these areas of government. The role of the Civil Service has been influential in the past, but the Ibbs report of 1988 [2] suggested a shift of emphasis towards greater ministerial control over policy, whilst the executive retain responsibility for implementation within either existing government departments or newly established next-step agencies.

Over the years, the government has sought to be more accountable for its actions, the Civil Service has always been monitored in its activities and parliamentary committees have been established to scrutinize and control the executive. For example, the Select Committee on the Environment acts as a watchdog over the town and country planning system.

WORKPIECE 4.1

ROLE OF CENTRAL GOVERNMENT

Using a country of your choice, show how the functions and responsibilties of central government are organized.

THE STRUCTURE OF THE CIVIL SERVICE

In order to operate effectively the Civil Service is organized into a series of departments, each having responsibility for particular issues. Within every department (overseen by a Secretary of State) there are a number of ministries, each under the control of a minister.

Virtually every government department has some influence, however small, over the environment. Policies for defence, for example, which result in a reduction in personnel within the armed forces will often mean the disposal of surplus land for other purposes, e.g. leisure or residential use. Changes in health policy to promote care in the community will encourage the change of use of many properties to provide such care.

One of the more influential departments regarding issues affecting both the built and natural environment is the Department of the Environment (DoE) which is responsible for the planning system in England. In 1992 it lost its responsibilities for heritage issues (for example, protection of buildings of special architectural or historic interest) to the Department of National Heritage (DNH). However, the DoE still retains its planning and development control functions. The recent creation of the Urban Development Agency has also removed some of the DoE roles regarding urban policy. Other areas, such as energy, which is the responsibility of the Department of Trade and Industry, and agricultural land, dealt with by the Ministry of Agriculture, Fisheries and Food (MAFF), are also outside the overall remit of the DoE. It is quite clear, however, that the policies and functions of these various departments impact frequently on one another. For example, proposals for sustainable development will often bring the DoE into direct conflict with MAFF.

It is necessary to consider in a little more detail the responsibilities of three of the more influential departments within the context of the built environment.

THE DEPARTMENT OF THE ENVIRONMENT (DoE)

This was established in 1970 under the control of the Secretary of State for the Environment, effectively giving this minister responsibility for a wide range of functions affecting society and the environment including housing, construction, planning, local government and transport. In Wales and Scotland these powers were assumed by the Secretaries of States for Wales and Scotland, respectively. Since its inception in 1970 the DoE has experienced several changes, including the removal of transport to the independent Department of Transport (DoT) in 1976 and the creation of a new Department of National Heritage in 1992.

As at September 1995, the DoE is divided into three separate ministries, each under a separate minister who is ultimately responsible to the Secretary of State. These are:

- Construction and Planning (which includes Energy Efficiency, Building Research Establishment and British Waterways Board);
- Local Government, Housing and Urban Regeneration;
- Environment and the Countryside (which includes Ordnance Survey).

The DoE, together with the DoT, has also developed a regional structure and hence is able to keep up to date with local issues and thus make more effective legislative and policy decisions.

DEPARTMENT OF TRANSPORT (DoT)   Since its establishment in 1976, this department has sought to maintain and enhance a high-quality system of transport. However, this has to be achieved having regard to issues of conservation and safety and must reflect the Government's Citizen's Charter, which refers to standards of public service provision. It must also make provision for all of society including the very young, the elderly and the disabled.

The DoT has responsibility for central government transport issues in England and has wider responsibilities across Britain including railways, the ports, airport policy and licence and taxation issues. These areas are dealt with by directorates within the DoT considering issues such as the Channel Tunnel, the road programme, public transport, etc. Divisions within each directorate address smaller but important policy issues, e.g. the Disability Unit.

DEPARTMENT OF NATIONAL HERITAGE (DNH)
Created in 1992 and known perhaps best for the National Lottery, the DNH has in fact taken some key planning functions from the DoE, such as heritage issues, and has taken over tourism policy from the Employment Department (now Department for Education and Employment).

Current responsibilities of the DNH include heritage and tourism, historic buildings and royal palaces, sport and the arts, and broadcasting and films. It now has responsibility for all listed buildings in England, of which there are about 450 000, and more than 13 000 ancient monuments. It also gives financial support to a wide range of conservation bodies. Perhaps the most widely known is English Heritage (previously Historic Buildings and Ancient Monuments Commission) which receives over £100 million annually, to be distributed to help maintain historic properties in its care or to provide grant aid to others.

AGENCIES

Inquiries into the management of government, reorganizations of departmental and ministerial responsibilities, and innovations in the control of public expenditure and in management have been a long-standing feature of British government. [3]

Delegation of power to a whole range of *ad hoc* agencies has been a feature of government decision making over many decades and their importance has grown considerably in recent years. These agencies may be external to government (quangos) or may operate within the machinery of government (next-step agencies).

WORKPIECE 4.2

KEY PLAYERS AND ENVIRONMENTAL ISSUES

Either individually or in groups, choose an environmental issue of national concern and make a list of the key players that have been involved in debating this issue.

QUANGOS

This term is defined as quasi-autonomous non-governmental organizations – in other words, agencies external to government. Whilst not directly part of the central government machine, they are controlled by government but at arm's length. They include bodies such as English Heritage, the Countryside Commission, English Nature, National Park authorities, urban development corporations and health authorities.

Many quangos were established during Mrs Thatcher's years as Prime Minister and were designed to take power away from local authorities, many of which were seen as inefficient by the government of the day. Whilst these agencies are established by central government and undertake various functions with rather wide discretionary powers, they remain outside the normal central/local government relationship. They are not democratically elected but they are directly funded by central government. The majority of members of quangos are appointed by the government.

The use of such delegation by government to establish agencies charged with such potentially wide-ranging powers, including plan making, implementation and enforcement, should encourage flexibility. It should allow these agencies to be responsive to the needs of communities at local level. In reality, however, they can become rather removed from public interests, often being influenced by various sectional interest groups both corporate and public in nature. They can be abolished at any time by the government and some are specifically established with only a limited life expectancy, e.g. the urban development corporations.

NEXT-STEP AGENCIES   More than 75 of these so-called executive agencies have been created since 1988 and more than 300 000 civil servants work within them. They operate on a strong basis of openness and accountability and their structure is very much based on a private sector operation. They are still, however, directly accountable to the minister whose department established them. There is a strong expectation that many of these next-step agencies will subsequently be privatized. The next step, therefore, is privatization!

Next-step agencies where output and outcomes are the focus rather than inputs include the Planning Inspectorate, the Land Registry and the Training and Employment Agency.

LEGISLATIVE ROLE OF CENTRAL GOVERNMENT

A particular feature of central government is its legislative role whereby new laws are created or law-making powers are delegated to a specified body or individual. Delegated or subordinate legislation has as much legal force as the Act that created it, provided that it operates within its powers – for example, the Town and Country Planning (General Permitted Development) Order 1995, SI No. 418 (discussed in Chapter 10).

Acts of Parliament evolve through a number of routes:

- public bills (government/select committee/private member);
- private bills;
- recommendations of the Law Commission.

PUBLIC BILLS

Matters that are relevant to the public generally may be enacted either by a government minister or by a private Member of Parliament.

GOVERNMENT BILLS

A government bill may be the result of party policy; for example, the Conservative Party election manifesto of the late 1970s led to the Housing Act 1980 provisions of 'right to buy' for council tenants. Alternatively, if circumstances dictate, legislation may be passed to address issues of national emergency or crisis. Standing committees are set up to consider the committee stage of any particular bill, such as amendments to clauses (Figure 4.1). They are then disbanded.

SELECT COMMITTEES

If the government requires a particular issue to be considered in depth, it may establish a Select Committee or set up a Royal Commission, such as the Royal Commission on Environmental Pollution (there have been numerous reports which have subsequently resulted in legislation, including the Control of Pollution Act 1974 and the Environmental Protection Act 1990). A Royal Commission reports directly to Parliament and normally will make proposals for legislation. There is, however, no legal requirement for the government to take up such recommendations. For example, the Report of the Layfield Commission on Local

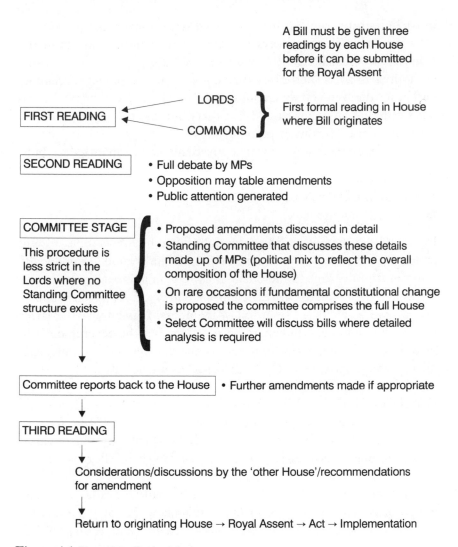

A Bill must be given three readings by each House before it can be submitted for the Royal Assent

FIRST READING ← LORDS / COMMONS } First formal reading in House where Bill originates

SECOND READING
• Full debate by MPs
• Opposition may table amendments
• Public attention generated

COMMITTEE STAGE

This procedure is less strict in the Lords where no Standing Committee structure exists

• Proposed amendments discussed in detail
• Standing Committee that discusses these details made up of MPs (political mix to reflect the overall composition of the House)
• On rare occasions if fundamental constitutional change is proposed the committee comprises the full House
• Select Committee will discuss bills where detailed analysis is required

Committee reports back to the House • Further amendments made if appropriate

THIRD READING

Considerations/discussions by the 'other House'/recommendations for amendment

Return to originating House → Royal Assent → Act → Implementation

Figure 4.1 Procedure for legislation.

Government 1976 contained recommendations on local government finance and the rating of properties, many of which were not accepted by the Labour government. Some Select Committees are a permanent feature of the House of Commons and retain individual membership for the life of a parliament, e.g. Committee on Privileges.

Whilst almost all public bills are successful, fewer than 30% of private members' bills become law [4]. This may be due to lack of time to debate, lack of discussion within Civil Service departments or, perhaps

PRIVATE MEMBERS'

BILLS

most important, the bill may not have strong government support. However, this is not always the case. For example, the Housing (Homeless Persons) Act 1977 which provided duties for local housing authorities to advise and assist the homeless, and to provide accommodation for them in certain circumstances, originated as a private member's bill (and an opposition MP at that) but was given parliamentary time and support by the government.

There are three ways in which private members can introduce bills:

- the ballot;
- Standing Order No. 39;
- the ten-minute rule.

In 1980–1985 there were 57 successful private members' bills, 75% of which were balloted, 19% under Standing Order 39 and 7% under the ten-minute rule. Private members' bills rely on guidance provided by clerks in the Public Bill Office, help from lobbying groups (where appropriate) and legal advice from fellow members. It is only at the latter stages when a bill looks likely to become law that the government will involve parliamentary counsel to review the drafting. Private members' bills are about one third of the length of government bills.

BALLOT BILLS   MPs holding no government position have an opportunity during each parliamentary session to enter a ballot for consideration of bills. Twenty names are drawn with only those whose names are drawn early having some likelihood of their bills ever becoming law.

Normally only 10 days in each session will be available for the debate of private members' bills and so it is likely that only the first six members in the ballot will see their bills reach a second reading. Whilst those MPs drawing high positions in the ballot may receive numerous suggestions from so-called private interest groups regarding suitable issues for law reform, it is more likely that the issue will be a government bill, a bill to enact the recommendations of some official law reform committee or body such as the Law Commission [4].

Research by D. Marsh and M. Read [4] indicated that during the period 1970–1985 there were 140 balloted bills:

- suggested to MPs by government and drafted by parliamentary counsel: 25%;
- based on recommendations of an official law committee: 29%;
- based on Law Commission reports: 9%;

- suggestions of interest groups: 11%;
- no origin known: 23%.

It thus seems clear that government support is a key issue in the success or failure of balloted bills.

STANDING ORDER 39 Whilst balloted bills will take up the vast majority of time allocated to debates on private members' bills, once the 20 balloted MPs have presented their bills then any other MP may, on giving one day's notice, present a bill to the House. Such a bill however can make no progress if there is any opposition to it, even if it is only one member. Needless to say, success using this route is less likely than through the ballot.

THE TEN-MINUTE RULE Each week any MP has the opportunity to make a speech of up to 10 minutes which supports the introduction of some new legislation (maximum of two speeches each week). If there is any opposition, a vote is taken to establish whether or not the bill should be read for the first time. If there is no opposition, a date is given for a second reading. Whilst this may seem to be an opportunity for those MPs unsuccessful in the ballot to drive through legislative changes, the constraints on time rarely allow the bill to proceed to the second reading unless there is no opposition and no requirement for the bill to be debated.

PRIVATE BILLS

These are normally used to deal with specific issues that may affect, for example, local authorities, nationalized industries, commercial undertakings, universities and other institutions. The procedure for private bills is rather different from public bills and is not dealt with in this text.

Examples of private bills include Midland Metro and Cardiff Bay Barrage. The length of time taken by private bills concerning issues relating to railways, trams, roads, canals and inland waterways was seen by some critics to be unacceptable. Procedures for dealing with such bills also gave cause for concern as they fail to allow expert assessors to be involved in considering technical evidence and hence influencing the final outcome. The result, after a process of report and consultations, was the 1992 Transport and Works Bill which indicated that proposals affecting inland waterways, diversions of rivers, canals and the like, light railway, tramway and underground railway schemes need no longer be the subject of a private Act of Parliament. Such schemes are now sanctioned by the use of a Works Order detailing the particular scheme and confirmed by the Secretary of State after procedures for publicity and public inquiry have been followed.

Where bills show features of both public and private bills, i.e. where the issue is of national importance but is contained within a specific local area, they are known as 'hybrid' bills. An example is the Channel Tunnel Bill 1986.

WORKPIECE 4.3

ACTS OF PARLIAMENT

Every year new laws are passed which affect our everyday lives. Choose an Act that has been evolved and describe what its impact is likely to be on you and the locality in which you live.

RECOMMENDATIONS OF THE LAW COMMISSION

The Law Commission was established in 1965 to make any necessary recommendations for legislative change. Such legal reform might include the repeal of statutes thought to be obsolete, the removal of anomalies, the codification of certain aspects of law or the consolidation of existing legislation.

Proposals presented to Parliament will frequently have draft bills attached but these will not necessarily be implemented.

POLICY

In addition to legislative powers, central government plays a major role in generating policy and guidance to local government, statutory undertakers, private developers and of course the public (Chapter 6). The Building Research Establishment, for example, gives a wide range of advice and information to the construction industry in this form of policy and guidance.

FUNDING

The funding arrangements made by central government clearly have a major role in determining development and investment decisions. In particular, the increasing provision of European funding for projects is of major significance. For example, European funding for infrastructure projects within some of the urban development corporation areas (e.g. Black Country and Cardiff Bay) has played a key role in determining policy and encouraging private sector investment. Central government financial policy decisions are particularly significant in determining local authority budget proposals (75% of local authority finance comes from the Exchequer) and hence the Finance Act that normally follows the Chancellor of the Exchequer's budget is of great significance. Similarly other policies have financial implications: money for housing improvement as opposed to new building, conservation rather than clearance, road improvement and public transport rather than new roads, will have a major influence on the built and natural environment and will often generate legislative control to support such policy.

It can be argued that it is of little benefit to society if rules are introduced but not enforced, and hence an important role of central government is to provide mechanisms for control which will allow compliance with policies and the proper implementation of both statutes and delegated legislation. In addition to the court system and alternatives for resolving disputes (Chapter 3) many government departments have systems whereby the Secretary of State (or perhaps a next-step agency) will have the final say regarding a policy issue. Redress through the courts must be on a point of law although the courts can intervene.

ENFORCEMENT

Many laws are seen as rather weak: they often fail to deal effectively with a particular activity, and enforcement appears somewhat limited. Special agencies may be entrusted with the responsibility of enforcement (e.g. the Health and Safety Executive) but often warnings or advice as opposed to prosecutions may be the most likely outcome.

Local and central government structures vary from country to country. In Britain there have been several attempts by central government since World War II to reorganize the structure of local government. At the time of writing, outside the major conurbations in England and Wales, the system is still largely based on that created by the Local Government Act 1972. In Scotland the system of local government was based on the Local Government (Scotland) Act 1973, which introduced a largely two-tier system with nine regional, 53 district and three island authorities. It would appear that there is a clearer distinction between the function of these authorities than currently exists in England and Wales.

LOCAL GOVERNMENT

The review of local government organizations in Britain has been undertaken concurrently by the DoE and the Welsh and Scottish Offices over the last few years. This will lead to some structural and boundary changes. In Wales the two-tier system has been completely replaced by unitary authorities and the same is about to occur in Scotland.

In England there are 39 county councils and within them 296 district councils in non-metropolitan areas. The abolition of the metropolitan councils by the Local Government Act of 1985 means there are a further 33 district councils and 36 London Borough Councils. Below district councils are parish councils (or community councils in Wales).

These county and district councils have a range of functions (Figure 4.2) which are governed by the various Local Government Acts. The responsibilities of counties include highways, education and social services; districts undertake responsibility for housing, rates, refuse collection and public health. Parish councils deal with a range of issues, including allotments, cemeteries and footpaths. Planning powers are shared between counties and districts.

Counties	Districts	Parish (Community)
Education	Housing	Bus shelters
Town and country planning shared with District Councils	Public health	Allotments
Social services	Refuse collection	Footpaths
Highways	Minor roads	Village greens/ burial grounds
Recreation and libraries	Rating	Parking places for motorcycles and bikes
Fire and police		

Figure 4.2 Responsibilities of local government.

Elections for all or part of the council occur on an annual basis. The public, through their democratic rights to vote, have a direct influence over the eventual 'political colour' of the council and hence its policies.

Whilst much of the local authority business will be dealt with at full council meetings, smaller committees are normally established and have powers delegated to them. These subcommittees should reflect the political balance of the full council. Examples will include the planning committee and the education committee. The recent attempt by government to ensure public awareness of local government activities via the Citizen's Charter has resulted in these subcommittee meetings being open to the public unless the council has resolved to meet 'in camera' in order to discuss an issue that would be prejudiced if publicity was given.

It is often suggested that a rather uneasy partnership exists between central and local government, with local government clearly having less power, being created through Acts of Parliament at central level and funded largely through central government grant.

Frequently policies between central and local government will differ if the respective parties are of different political colour. Lack of central government funding may cause local authorities to set illegal budgets (for example, Shropshire County Council in 1995) and some central government policies, including those relating to the sale of council houses, may be largely ignored.

Local government is bound by the doctrine of 'ultra vires'; that is, authorities are only permitted to undertake activities for which they have statutory authority. Clearly the range of activities undertaken by local authorities is extremely diverse. Section 111 of the Local Government Act 1972 empowers local authorities to do 'anything which is reasonably incidental to their authorized activities and designed to facilitate the discharge of any of their functions'. If individuals are of the opinion that a local authority is acting in excess of its powers they can apply to the courts for judicial review. How often is action taken by individuals against local authorities?

The cost of applying to the courts and the procedures required may discourage many people from seeking redress, but there is an alternative: the local government ombudsman. Overseen by the Commission for Local Administration, these local commissioners investigate complaints of maladministration and then make a report to the local authority concerned. They have no powers to order or award compensation but local authorities are under a duty to consider any report made by the commissioner and reply as to their proposed course of action. This seems to be a useful vehicle to monitor and control local government activity.

LINKS BETWEEN CENTRAL AND LOCAL GOVERNMENT

WORKPIECE 4.4

LOCAL GOVERNMENT OMBUDSMAN

Either individually or in groups, make a list of the types of cases that may be heard by the local government ombudsman.

THE PUBLIC

Our democratic system currently elects a central government based on the principle of 'first past the post' in each constituency. Whilst proportional representation may have its merits, it has been discussed and discarded to date by both the main political parties. However, the existence of a number of different political parties in Parliament ensures that no single party can entirely control the policies of the nation. Acts are often seen as political compromises with the public involvement occurring at election time and through the lobbying of MPs regarding both government bills and private members' bills. It has been suggested that it is the more powerful classes and interest groups that influence legislation, often failing to recognize the disbenefits to others if the benefits to themselves are seen to be substantial [5].

Public opinion does seem to be a rather general term which in fact frequently reflects the view of a rather select group of society and it is therefore almost impossible to identify a single 'public interest'. It is true to say that much of the legislation produced during each parliamentary session is uncontentious, with some working for the benefit of the less well-off members of society (e.g. local authority services and welfare initiatives), but on other occasions the voices of perhaps the more vociferous minorities may promote schemes for cuts in public sector spending, and shifts from public to private sector investment. The result suggests a reality which is not quite what the 'democratic doctor' ordered.

INTEREST GROUPS

Given the fact that with a predominance of government bills there will be much debate and consultation outside Parliament itself, the importance of interest groups in putting forward views on various legislative proposals should not be underestimated. Some groups exist permanently to represent their interests regarding specific issues. These include the Country Land Owners Association (CLA), SAVE Britain's Heritage, the Confederation of British Industry (CBI), the National Housebuilders Federation (NHF), Friends of the Earth, the Civic Trust, the National Trust, and the Council for the Protection of Rural England (CPRE), which are all examples of non-governmental organizations (NGOs) who are extremely influential over government policy but are autonomous.

Not all interest groups exist on a permanent basis. Many will be established merely as pressure groups to campaign for particular issues, often being disbanded when the issue has been resolved – for example, 'Ban the Wharf' in Brightlingsea, Essex, and 'Stop the Bypass' in Knowle, West Midlands.

INTEREST GROUPS

Make a list of five local and five national interest groups.
Give an example of how an interest group might influence legislation and policy.

Support for greater public awareness regarding environmental issues is also being provided by European legislation (see below). For example, the 1990 EC directive on Freedom of Access to Information on the Environment will enable pressure groups to adopt a watchdog role over public bodies.

It is hoped that, by heightening public awareness of environmental issues, public and private sector bodies will be encouraged to 'put their house in order' or force the consequences of people 'voting with their feet'. To date the use of such environmental registers by the general public is still rather low.

The UK's membership of the European Economic Community (EEC), now European Union (EU), came as a result of the 1972 European Communities Act. Over the last 20 years or so the EU has become a major influence in terms of policy and control, particularly in areas of economic and environmental concern. It is likely that this influence will increase over the coming years.

The EU is an extremely complex structure both politically and organizationally. It comprises a parliament to which each member state elects members, but essentially this body is supervisory and advisory. Policy making in the EU is undertaken by the Council of Ministers, usually based on proposals of the European Commission. These are normally senior members, often foreign ministers, of the member states. 'It is this Council that makes Community Laws, known as Regulations, which are binding on Member States' [3]. The Council also issues Directives which are also binding but are implemented by legislation within each of the member states. 'Decisions' issued by the Council are 'binding on the member state organization, firm or individual to whom they are addressed'.

It is evident, therefore, that the Parliament at Westminster is now bound by EU legislation and its role as the supreme law-making authority within the UK has been eroded. European Union law prevails over UK Acts of Parliament and delegated legislation.

THE EUROPEAN UNION (EU)

Whilst the role of the European Commission is largely concerned with the development of proposals for consideration by the Council of Ministers, it also has powers to deal with infringements of EU law. If the Commission is unable to resolve a particular issue it will refer the matter to the European Court of Justice whose decision will then be legally binding.

Across Europe the constitution regulates the organization of the state in terms of its legislative and executive roles and the functions of organizations and individuals that hold power, including the president, prime minister, government and parliament. Proposals for new laws are normally discussed and voted upon in Parliament and often emanate from the Ministry of Justice. Chapter 5 provides further detail on the influence of the European Union on the built environment.

SUMMARY

As society becomes more complex, so it requires an increasing range of policies and legal controls to ensure that it operates in an efficient and fair manner. Such control mechanisms and policies are the responsibilty of a wide range of organizations operating both within and across national boundaries and these in turn elicit a response from many other groups and individuals to create the legal framework currently operating across the built environment.

This chapter has:

- identified the key players;
- examined their role in responding to and generating control and policy;
- discussed how laws are made;
- considered how the role of the European Union is increasing.

CHECKLIST

- The law has been influenced by many 'players'.
- Central government plays a major role.
- Policy is formulated by the Cabinet.
- Parliament carries out the framing of laws.
- The Civil Service administers the system through the various government departments.
- Power has been delegated to a number of quangos and next-step agencies in recent years.
- New laws evolve via public bills, private bills, hybrid bills or recommendations of the Law Commission.
- Local government has a wide range of functions governed by the various Acts of Parliament.

- Local government is bound by the doctrine of 'ultra vires'.
- The public makes a significant contribution to the debate surrounding election of the ruling parties and hence policy and legislative decisions.
- The EU is playing an increasing role in terms of policy and control in a wide range of economic and environmental issues.

REFERENCES

1. Ryden, Y. (1993) *The British Planning System*, Macmillan.
2. Ibbs, B. (1990) *House of Commons Services*, HMSO.
3. Cullingworth, J.B. and Nadin, V. (1994) *Town and Country Planning in Britain*, 11th edn, Routledge.
4. Zander, M. (1990) *The Law Making Process*, 3rd edn, Weidenfeld and Nicholson.
5. Dicey, A.V. (1959) *The Law of the Constitution*, 10th edn (ed. E.C.S. Wade), Butterworths.

FURTHER READING

Edward, D. and Lane, R. (1995) *European Community Law (An Introduction)*, Butterworths.

Galbraith, A. and Stockdale, M. (1993) *Building and Land Management Law for Students*, 3rd edn, Butterworth–Heinemann.

Hoan, N., Kotz, H. and Leser, H. (1982) *German Private and Commercial Law*, Clarendon.

THE INFLUENCE OF THE EUROPEAN UNION ON THE BUILT ENVIRONMENT

DAVID LYNCH

THEME

Over the last 10 years, with the passing of the Single European Act and the Treaty on European Union, European law has had an increasing impact on the legislative system of the UK. So, what are the functions of the European Union? How do they affect the UK? This chapter seeks to de-mystify the European Union by examining the legislative process and policies that have had an impact on the built environment.

OBJECTIVES

After reading this chapter you should be able to:

● understand the European Union legislative process;

● understand the development and functions of the European Union institutions;

● make comparisons between the European and UK legislative systems;

● consider the impact of the European Union on the built environment.

INTRODUCTION

The British system of law and government is now essentially part of a wider European system. European legislation and policies have a direct influence on built environment professionals, and the built environment is itself being changed physically by the policies of the European Union. As at April 1995, there were 15 member states in the European Union and this number is likely to continue to grow. Policy decisions and legislative controls issued by the EU will continue to play a key role in influencing the development of Britain's built and natural environment, whether through the provision of financial support for projects, the reduction or removal of trading constraints, policies for agriculture, environmental controls or political change. What is abundantly clear is that, for the future, increasing emphasis will be placed on the European Union and as such it is an area that requires further study.

In the historical development of Europe, legislative systems and the built environment are closely linked. Europe has developed, to the extent that most of its citizens now live within the built environment. The modern political, economic and urban systems as we know them had their beginnings in a European context through the city states of Ancient Greece, and were later influenced through the political and legal system of the Roman Empire.

The model of the city as an economic centre developed during the Middle Ages through the expansion of the merchant towns. During the Renaissance the cities grew as they became centres of trade and wealth, not only through trading within Europe, but through the beginnings of colonial expansion. In the northern European cities such as Amsterdam and Bruges, the modern market economy evolved in order to finance this expanding system of global trade. This circle of growth with wealth flowing back to the towns meant an expansion of the built environment.

The growth in trade extended beyond the European continent and the Mediterranean. With the establishment of the Dutch East India Company, the era of colonial expansion began. Industry in European cities grew, in part, to deal with the new raw materials from the colonies, such as cotton. The infrastructure needs of trade led to the technological changes in the eighteenth century and the industrial revolution. The built environment rapidly grew and changed through the growth of industry and the influx of labour from the countryside to the towns to serve that industry. At this time there was no effective legal system to regulate and control this growth of industry. The new cities created by the industrial revolution generated wealth but created pollution, poverty, poor housing and disease.

The concept of *laissez-faire* and free enterprise implied no state involvement. The factories were free to pollute the rivers and the

THE DEVELOPMENT OF THE EUROPEAN BUILT ENVIRONMENT

builders were not constrained from building poorly lit, ill-ventilated slums. For the mass of people in the first two thirds of the nineteenth century, freedom meant the freedom to live in squalor. [1]

The crisis of poverty and decline in public health led to the built environment coming under a regulatory framework. In the late nineteenth century the UK government passed social legislation to improve public health and to regulate industry and the work environment. The industrial revolution led to the growth of new cities such as Birmingham and the extension of a legal system to local authorities. These new councils intervened directly in the built environment both to improve social conditions and to build new city centres.

The economic depression of the 1930s created a degradation of the urban environment in traditional industrial areas all over Europe. Then World War II devastated the built environment of Europe in the industrial areas of Belgium, Holland, Germany, France and the UK.

WORKPIECE 5.I

SOURCES OF EUROPEAN INFORMATION

Up-to-date information is important for built environment professionals, if they are to take advantage of the opportunities that Europe offers. You will need to know where to find information from a variety of sources. Identify:

- the nearest European Documentation centre;
- the nearest European Information centre;

- the office of your local Member of the European Parliament;
- the UK offices of the European Parliament and the European Commission.

Make a list of the range of information that can be found in a European Documentation centre.

POST-WAR RECONSTRUCTION

After World War II, the Iron Curtain divided Europe into two blocs. The Soviet Union influenced Eastern and Central Europe, while the United States and its allies influenced Western Europe. The enormous scale of the task to reconstruct the post-war European built environment would demand different legal, political and economic systems. The problems were too great for individual cities or countries to deal with: an international solution had to be found. The Marshall Aid Plan (involving funding from the United States) assisted the urban and economic regeneration of Western Europe in the immediate post war years.

In 1951, during the Paris Summit of Western political leaders, it was recognized that there would have to be a pan-European solution to the problem of the economic reconstruction of Europe. The summit created the European Coal and Steel Community (ECSC). The aim of the Community was to enable the steel and coal industry in the Saar and Ruhr areas of France and Germany to produce the raw products for economic and environmental reconstruction. So right from the start, the first European Community was concerned with the built environment. The Messina Summit in 1955 led to the creation of the Treaty of Rome in 1957. The six countries of France, Germany, Italy, Belgium, Luxembourg and the Netherlands created the European Economic Community and the European Atomic Energy Community. The Community had a legal framework and was aimed at the economic success of Europe through an ever-closer union of the peoples of Europe.

GROWTH OF THE EUROPEAN ECONOMIC COMMUNITY (EEC)

In order to carry out the legal programme of the Treaty of Rome a multi-national legislative system had to be created. In the 1960s the institutions of the EEC were formed: the Commission as a technical bureaucracy to draft European legislation; the Council of Ministers to pass European Laws; and the European Assembly and Economic and Social Committee to give opinions on proposed legislation. The European Court of Justice was created to arbitrate, enforce and interpret the Treaty law. In 1972 the Brussels treaty led to the first enlargement of the Community, when Ireland, the United Kingdom and Denmark joined.

The European legislative process continued in 1979 with the first direct elections to the European Parliament and there was now a directly elected and democratic input to the EEC. Greece became the tenth member of the Community in 1982.

THE EUROPEAN COMMUNITY AND THE SINGLE MARKET

An important year was 1986, when Portugal and Spain joined the Community – which meant that the EEC was an enlarged community where most of the populations lived in the built environment. There were great disparities in wealth and urban conditions, particularly between northern Europe and the southern and peripheral regions of Europe. There was a major shift in the emphasis of the Community. The EEC was essentially a trading bloc and could not deal with these inequalities. In order to develop into a single market of 12 countries there would have to be a legislative framework that could cope with the great volume of law that would need to be passed to ensure that the single market would be operational on a fair, level playing field in all member states. Thus the Single European Act, which amended the Treaty of Rome, was passed. The next few years until the end of 1992 were aimed at creating a single European market, and closing the gap between the richer and poorer regions of the European Community.

THE CREATION OF THE EUROPEAN UNION (EU)

The move to an ever closer union of the peoples of Europe as envisaged in the Treaty of Rome was advanced during discussions at the Intergovernmental Conferences of Brussels and Maastricht in 1991/92. This led to the signing of the Treaty on European Union, better known as the Maastricht Treaty. This treaty further amended the Treaty of Rome and created the European Union.

SOURCES OF EUROPEAN UNION LAW

Over time the member states have granted the European Union legal powers. What are the primary sources of such powers and how are they enacted?

THE TREATIES

These are the primary source of EU law, and define the competencies of the EU and the powers of the institutions. These powers are known as the Acquis Communautaire. The treaty can be amended only by the member states acting in unanimity at an intergovernmental conference. Treaties become law on ratification by member states and there are no derogations or opt-outs from the treaty unless agreed before the treaty is ratified. The United Kingdom's opt-outs from the Social Chapter and Economic and Monetary Union from the Maastricht Treaty are current examples [2]. A treaty applies equally to member states, organizations and private individuals.

THE TREATY OF ROME 1957　The Treaty of Rome was the founding treaty of the European Economic Community. It created a single community including the EEC, the European Atomic Energy Community and the European Coal and Steel Community (ECSC). The Treaty was modified by the Single European Act 1986.

THE SINGLE EUROPEAN ACT 1986　The main aim of this treaty revision was to create a single European market by the end of 1992, carried out by implementing the 'four freedoms':

1.　the free movement of goods;
2.　the free movement of services;
3.　the free movement of capital;
4.　the free movement of people.

The European Parliament gained wider powers of co-decision on legislation with the EU's Council of Ministers. The Act aimed to speed up the legislative process in order to get through the sheer volume of technical and enabling legislation needed to create the single market. The process was also assisted by the end of the right of veto by one country, on single market legislation, at the Council of Ministers.

TREATY ON EUROPEAN UNION 1992   The aim of this treaty was to create a European Union which included social, political and economic elements. Thus it creates the legal concept of European citizenship, extends the freedom to move and work and recognizes vocational, academic and professional qualifications. The legal principle of **subsidiarity** was introduced. This meant that decisions should be taken at the appropriate legislative level – either European, national, regional or local. To enable the completion of the single market, Economic and Monetary Union (EMU) – in other words, the single currency – was proposed. The Treaty also extended powers relating to foreign policy, justice and home affairs and consolidated social provision. The European Parliament was given a greater role in deciding legislation through powers of co-decision with the Council [3].

WORKPIECE 5.2

POWERS OF GOVERNMENT

Subsidiarity means taking decisions at the most appropriate level of government. Find out the powers that each level of government has in:

- Europe

- United Kingdom
- Local authorities.

Do they share any powers?
Would you restrict or add any powers to Europe?

SECONDARY LEGISLATION

European secondary legislation, based on the principle of the Acquis Communautaire, cannot change, amend, act contrary to or repeal provisions made in a treaty. All secondary legislation must have a legal basis in a treaty. For example, the provision of public housing is not in the Treaty, and therefore there can be no secondary legislation that creates a European public housing policy. Secondary legislation follows one of four forms: regulations, decisions, directives and opinions/recommendations.

REGULATIONS   Regulations are uniformly applied throughout the EU 20 days after being published. They apply to member states and EU citizens equally. A regulation is binding in its entirety, it has to be directly applied and it automatically becomes part of a member state's legal system. EU regulations have priority over existing national laws and regulations and apply mainly to day-to-day agricultural measures such as milk quotas, produce prices and import quotas. A regulation may also need to be used for international sanctions such as those taken against Iraq during the Gulf War. It is quite clear that regulations applying to agriculture have had, and will continue to have, a considerable effect on the environment, and farmers seek to diversify in an attempt to make better use of land and buildings rendered inefficient by European quotas.

DIRECTIVES   The secondary legislation is enforced through use of member states' own legislative processes. Directives in the UK are implemented through Parliament. There is some room for interpretation within the legal framework of the directive and it is binding only if the ends to be achieved leave the means of implementation to the member states. Member states have a period (usually two years) in which to implement the directive. The majority of directives are aimed at producing common European standards (for example, in environmental legislation) and single market measures. An example of environmental legislation relevant to the built environment is the Environmental Impact Directive [4]. Here developers seeking planning permission for particular types of scheme are required to provide environmental impact assessments for consideration as part of the planning application.

DECISIONS   A decision may be binding, with legal effect, or informal and non-binding in member states. The essential element of a decision is that it is directed to a member state, regional organization or individual, but it is not a general piece of legislation. An example in the built environment sphere is in the field of European Regional Policy and structural funds of that policy (the structural funding policy is discussed in the later section on 'Europe, the built environment and regional policy'). An individual European funding programme, such as the operational programme in Birmingham, is based on a Community Decision, for example [5].

RECOMMENDATIONS AND OPINIONS   These have no legal force and are purely concerned with setting out guidelines on how to carry out a policy or legislation.

OTHER SOURCES OF EU LAW

The judgments of the European Court of Justice are binding only on individual cases, and there is no rule of precedent for following cases. However, judgments do have implications in related or similar cases. In practice, judgments have a moral authority and tend not to be conflicting with one another. An example of this was the 1989 Titanium Dioxide case [6] and the result of this case meant that the same legislative process was applied in subsequent European environmental legislation.

European law follows generally accepted international principles, such as the protection of human rights and equality before the law.

The EU is also bound by public international law, such as international maritime law. It has the power, on behalf of the member states, to enter into international agreements or treaties with Third World countries. Examples include the Basel Convention on the transportation of waste, and the Montreal Convention on the depletion of the ozone layer by CFCs.

To understand how the European legislative process works, it is essential to understand the functions of the European institutions within this process. It is also important to understand the component parts of the legislative process in a European context.

A legislative system consists of the powers and functions exercised by the executive, the legislature and the judiciary. Clear-cut legislative functions are not well defined in Europe.

- The **executive** functions of the EU are shared by the Commission and the Council of Ministers.
- The **legislature** is made up of the Council of Ministers, who debate and vote on European legislation, and the European Parliament, which has a role close to that of the US Senate or the House of Lords. This role is essentially that of a scrutinizing second chamber.
- The **judiciary** consists of the European Commission, which has to ensure that European laws are being applied by the member states, and also the European Court of Justice, which interprets and enforces European law.
- The functions of the fourth arm of government, the **Civil Service**, are carried out mainly by the Commission, as well as the secretariats of the various European institutions.

THE EUROPEAN LEGISLATIVE SYSTEM

The European Council is made up of the heads of government of the member states. Its role is to set the political and legislative agenda, as well as to change or amend the treaties, as in Maastricht, for example. The Council is run by a Presidency that rotates every six months between each head of government. For example, from June to December 1992,

THE EUROPEAN COUNCIL

John Major and the UK government held the Presidency. This enables each member state to set the political agenda. The Council is also responsible for external relations with other countries outside the EU.

THE COUNCIL OF MINISTERS

The Council of Ministers consists of ministers from each of the member states and membership varies according to the subject under consideration. For example, the Environment Council is made up of all 15 environment ministers from the member states, and is chaired by the minister whose country currently holds the Presidency of the European Council. The Council of Ministers is the primary legislative body; it takes decisions and passes EU laws. The Council is assisted by national civil servants, who are based in Brussels and are known as the Committee of Permanent Representatives (COREPER). The civil servants who assist UK ministers, and are based in the UK embassy to the European Union, are collectively known as UKREP.

THE COMMISSION OF THE EUROPEAN COMMUNITY

The Commission is both the guardian of the Treaty of Rome and the bureaucracy. It consists of 20 Commissioners who are nominated by the individual national governments of the member states. The larger countries such as Germany, France, Italy, Spain and the UK have two Commissioners each; the rest have one each. They are independent from the member states and on taking office swear an oath of independence from member states. Each of the Commissioners has a five-year term of office and has a policy portfolio. The UK has appointed Neil Kinnock and Leon Brittan as Commissioners. Commissioner Kinnock was given the responsibility for transport, and Commissioner Brittan the responsibility for external trade relations. The portfolios are allocated by the President of the Commission, who is chosen by the European Council.

The Commissioners are responsible for the 23 000 staff who make up the administration of the Commission and these staff are split into departments known as Directorate Generals (DGs). For example, DG XI (11) is responsible for the administration of environment policy. Each DG is headed by a senior administrator known as the Director-General. There are also other departments such as research, media relations, and the joint translation and interpretation service.

The Commission has several functions. It initiates policies and is responsible for the technical drafting of legislation. It acts on behalf of the EU against member states if they fail to fulfil their treaty obligations. The Commission is responsible for the monitoring and enforcing of legislation and also for the day-to-day administration of the EU. The Commission spends the EU budget and allocates funds from the various budget lines.

The judicial function of the Commission is to ensure that EU laws are correctly applied in all member states; hence it has powers of investigation and detection, and can initiate enforcement proceedings against a Member State.

The European Parliament is made up of 626 members (MEPs), who are directly elected from each member state. The European elections take place every five years. MEPs sit in cross-national political groups. For example, the largest political group in the 1994–1999 Parliament is the group of the party of European Socialists; Labour MEPs are members of this group. Conservative MEPs and a Unionist MEP sit with the European People's Party (Christian Democrats). Liberal Democrat MEPs are part of the European Liberal, Democratic and Reform Group, and Scottish Nationalist MEPs are members of the European Radical Alliance. Ian Paisley, a Northern Ireland MEP, sits as an independent. The political groups are important as all resources for political administrative staff, committee places, reports and speaking time are allocated on a pro rata basis according to the number of MEPs in each group. This is to maintain the political balance of the Parliament.

The Parliament works on a similar basis to a UK local authority and clearly has influential powers. It operates on a monthly cycle. In the first two weeks the standing committees debate reports on the legislation; for example, all environmental legislation and policies will be dealt with by C11, the committee on the environment, public health and consumer affairs. The committees meet in Brussels. In week three the political groups meet in Brussels to prepare their voting positions on the agenda for the full session of Parliament. In the fourth week Parliament meets in plenary session in Strasbourg. Here the legislation and reports are voted on by the full Parliament. The Parliament is assisted by its civil service: the Secretariat, which is based in Luxembourg. Due to its increased workload the Parliament also meets occasionally in Brussels for part-sessions.

POWERS AND RIGHTS OF THE EUROPEAN PARLIAMENT The Parliament can compel the whole Commission to resign and has the right to endorse a new Commission, as it did early in 1995. The Parliament has gained several legislative powers. Its legitimacy

THE EUROPEAN PARLIAMENT

Political Group	MEPs
Group of the Party of European Socialists	221
European People's Party (Christian Democrats)	173
Union for Europe Group	56
European Liberal, Democratic and Reform Group	53
European Unitarian Left	30
Green Group	25
European Radical Alliance	19
Nations of Europe	19
Independents	31

Source: European Parliament

Figure 5.1 Political composition of the European Parliament (July 1995).

is to express the political will of European citizens who elected them. It has the right to give its opinion on legislation and in some cases amend, veto or delay legislation. On some legislation it has powers of co-decision with the Council of Ministers. The Parliament has the right to set the EU budget along with the Council of Ministers. It has the right to agree to the accession of new countries. It can investigate maladministration through the Ombudsman. It has the right to question the Council and the Commission. It can set up Committees of Inquiry on important issues.

The role of the European Parliament should not be underestimated and hence the election of MEPs is of considerable importance to all the member states.

THE EUROPEAN COURT OF JUSTICE

The European Court of Justice is made up of 16 judges and six advocates general, who are lawyers appointed by the member states. Like the Commission, they are independent of the member states, and they serve for a six-year term. The Court is based in Luxembourg and sits in a plenary session of all the judges and advocates general or in smaller chambers of three to five judges. The function of the Court is to give a reasoned submission on the cases before it. The Court ensures observance of EU law and is responsible for the interpretation and application of the Treaty.

The Court of the First Instance is a part of the Court that deals with EU staff cases and actions in competition law, anti-dumping law and the ECSC Treaty.

THE ECONOMIC AND SOCIAL COMMITTEE

This body is made up of members nominated by the member states and currently the UK has 24 representatives. The members comprise employers' organizations, trade unions and voluntary organizations. The Committee has the right to be consulted over proposed legislation.

THE COMMITTEE OF THE REGIONS

This Committee has exactly the same rights as the Economic and Social Committee but its members are appointed from local government throughout the EU. Again the UK has 24 members, made up of councillors from local authorities.

WORKPIECE 5.3

COMPARISON OF LEGISLATIVE SYSTEMS IN EUROPE

In this chapter you have looked at the legislative system of the European Union in comparison with the United Kingdom and the United States.

Find out how the legislative systems of two other EU countries work. How are the powers of the executive, legislature and judiciary organized? In what ways are they different from or similar to the European Union?

THE LEGISLATIVE PROCESS

The legislative process of the European Union consists of four stages: initiation; opinion and scrutiny; decision; and implementation (Figure 5.2).

INITIATION   The legislative proposal is drafted by the Commission. It may well consult with outside bodies, technical experts and pressure groups.

OPINION AND SCRUTINY   The proposal is sent to the Economic and Social Committee and the Committee of the Regions for consultation. They send their opinion to the Commission. The proposal is also sent to the Council of Ministers and the European Parliament. The Parliament gives a formal opinion to the Commission via scrutiny of the proposed legislation in committees and full parliamentary session.

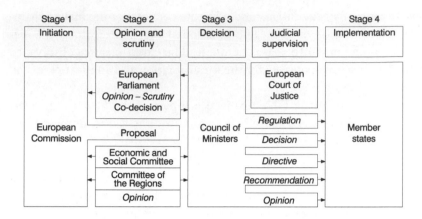

Figure 5.2 How European laws are passed.

DECISION   The Parliament can accept, reject or amend the proposal. If it is accepted it is voted on by the Council of Ministers. Rejection or amendment by the Parliament leads to negotiations between the Council of Ministers, the Commission and the Parliament. The Parliament then has a second reading of the changed proposal to accept, reject or amend. If accepted at this stage it is voted on by the Council of Ministers. If it is rejected again by the Parliament, the proposal falls or can only be agreed by an unanimous vote at the Council of Ministers.

QUALIFIED MAJORITY VOTING

Qualified majority voting (Figure 5.3) was a procedure introduced to speed up decision making by the Council of Ministers. Most of the legislation dealing with the single market and provisions is dealt with under the Maastricht Treaty. Before qualified majority voting, all legislation could be vetoed by an individual member state. The procedure works by giving each country a weighted vote according to the size of the population. Therefore a proposal can only be blocked if several countries are against it.

WORKPIECE 5.4

LOBBYING

Imagine that the European Commission is going to bring forward a directive in the field of environmental policy that will have a negative impact for built environment professionals. Devise a strategy to lobby the European Union to stop this directive.

- What process will the directive go through?
- Which organizations will you need to talk to?
- At what point in the process will you contact each organization?
- Who could support you and who might be against you?

Votes (each)	Countries
10	Germany, France, Italy, United Kingdom
8	Spain
5	Belgium, Greece, Netherlands, Portugal
3	Denmark, Ireland, Finland
2	Luxembourg

Figure 5.3 Qualified majority voting. Each country has a weighted vote according to its size.

The Commission is responsible for policing legislation. What happens if there is a breach of legislation by one of the member states? Article 169 letters are sent to member states if they fail to implement EU laws. If an Article 169 letter is ignored, the Commission takes the member state to the European Court of Justice for a breach of the Treaty (Article 171). The Court can fine the member state under the Maastricht Treaty.

The European Court of Justice deals with four sorts of cases:

- failure to fulfil treaty obligations by a member state (where a member state fails to implement legislation, such as failing to implement a directive within the time period);
- failure of institutions to act (where an institution fails to fulfil its functions under the Treaty);
- referrals from national courts for preliminary rulings (national courts can refer some cases to the Court of Justice for a ruling concerning European laws);
- claims for damages against the EU.

JUDICIAL SUPERVISION AND ENFORCEMENT

The primary purpose of the European Steel and Coal Community was to intervene directly in the built environment, through the restructuring of the urban economy. This approach of intervention in the built environment by the EU has remained a constant part of the European political and legislative agenda. The direct impact of the European Union on the built environment can be clearly seen through the development of European regional policy and the 'structural funds'. The legal framework was established in 1975, and the European Regional Development Fund (ERDF) initiated a programme of funding to bring about the convergence of the regions of Europe. The increase in legislation and the need to speed up the process of the single market meant that regional conver-

EUROPE, THE BUILT ENVIRONMENT AND REGIONAL POLICY

gence was of more importance. In 1988 the structural funds were reformed so that they would be targeted on problems and areas in most need.

Many regions in the UK have benefited from infrastructure developments, such as Merseyside and the West Midlands. Built environment professionals have been very closely involved in this policy process, particularly in its local delivery. The objective funding is only a part of the regional policy, and the next phase will be to create trans-European networks to include physical links such as transport, and telecommunication and information 'super-highways'.

SINGLE MARKET MEASURES

The free movement of goods, capital, services and people has direct implications for the built environment. For the first time in the development of the built environment, a project in one country may now receive financing from a second country and be designed and built by professionals in a third. An example of the change is the mutual recognition of qualifications. Surveyors are an integral part of the development of the built environment in the UK, but in continental Europe no similar profession exists in its own right. However, with single market legislation there is an opening in Europe and indeed the professional body (The Royal Institution of Chartered Surveyors) now has a European office in Brussels and is expanding the profession in Europe, creating a market niche. Free movement should mean that built environment professionals will have their qualifications recognized and be free to practise throughout the European Union. It will be interesting to see how quickly this will happen and on what scale.

PUBLIC PROCUREMENT

The single market and resulting legislation opened up public procurement, or contracts for public bodies such as local or national governments and the European institutions. Now big contracts such as development, provision of service and tenders for supply of goods have to be advertised on a European level. Any organization or individual in the EU may put in a bid for the contract, and clearly there are opportunities for built environment professions to take advantage of this new market.

EU AND THE FUTURE

There is a wide range of views on how the European Union should develop. On your own, make a list of:

- the strengths and weaknesses of the European Union legislative system;
- the future opportunities that might face Europe;

- the potential threats to the development of the European Union.

In a group of three to four, compare your lists. How were the lists different?

SUMMARY

As Europe developed its built environment the legislative system developed alongside. The growth in stages from the Greek city states to merchant cities and nation states has meant a growth in the legislative system to cope with the problems that the urban environment creates. After the European built environment had been changed by World War II, pan-national systems were needed to deal with the rebuilding of Europe.

The legislative framework of the EEC grew as the Community developed to become the European Union in 1992. As the individual member states granted more powers by amending the Treaty of Rome, the European institutions grew and gained new powers. The legislative system has influenced built environment and as the powers of Europe have grown, its impact on the built environment has increased.

CHECKLIST

This chapter has:

- considered the development of Europe and its impact on the built environment;
- developed an understanding of the elements of a legislative system in a European context;
- outlined the legislative processes of the European Union.

REFERENCES

1. Short, J. (1984) *An Introduction to Urban Geography*, Routledge & Kegan Paul, pp. 11–12 and 15.
2. Council and Commission of the European Community (1992) *The Treaty on European Union*, EEC, Luxembourg, pp. 76–78 and 191–201.
3. European Commission (1992) *European Community Environment Legislation*, Vol. 1, pp. 30–47, General Policy, EEC Council Directive 83/337/EEC of 27 June 1985, EEC, Luxembourg.
4. European Commission (1992) *The Communty's Structural Interventions*, No. 4, EEC, Luxembourg, p. 37.

5. European Commission (1992) *European Community Environment Legislation*, Vol. 2, EEC, Luxembourg, p. 22, General Policy, EEC Council Directive 89/428/EEC.

6. Case 300/89, *Commission* v. *Council* [1991].

FURTHER READING

Jacobs, F. and Corbett, R. (1995) *The European Parliament*, 3rd edn, Longman.

Old Bailey Press (1993) *European Community Law.* An *overview*, 3rd edn, Old Bailey Press.

Wyatt, D. and Dashwood, A. (1993) *European Community Law*, Sweet & Maxwell.

POLICY AND PROCEDURES

JEAN BADMAN AND LAURIE GRIMMETT

Legislation, and delegated legislation, is invariably a reflection of government policy. Policy also influences the interpretation of legislation and delegated legislation after enactment, and offers guidance on procedures to be adopted. Policies may be issued in various ways by government at both central and local level. These include 'rules', standard codes of practice, guidelines, circulars, guidance notes, White and Green Papers, departmental publications, ministerial statements and answers in Parliament. The courts at times also have their own views over policy. This chapter considers these issues.

THEME

After reading this chapter you should be able to:

OBJECTIVES

- be aware of the wide range of central government policy documents;

- understand the distinction between Green and White Papers;

- appreciate the role played by Circulars in implementing central government policy;

- understand the significance of planning, mineral and regional policy guidance to the built environment;

- appreciate the influence which judges may exercise on public policy.

Governments pass legislation and subordinate legislation, but it is not always appropriate or practical for all issues to be dealt with in this man-

INTRODUCTION

ner. Frequently there may be a need to produce policy documents, codes of practice or other technical standards which are intended to provide guidance for both the private and public sector but do not necessarily have the 'force of law'. This may be due to the need to allow some discretion or flexibility. In some cases policy documents pre-empt legislation and administrative rules become embodied in Civil Service and local authority practice. So what are these 'rules' and guidance documents? This chapter looks at some of the more significant aspects of policy and procedure.

CENTRAL GOVERNMENT POLICY

The so-called rules of administrative practice (rather than legal rules) are sometimes described as quasi-legislation. They are intended to act as a regulator for statutory and discretionary powers of government. Not all quasi-legislative rules, whereby an administration can introduce specific policies into the use of discretionary powers, are published. Some are privately notified to the bodies concerned whilst others may be kept secret within the administration. Clearly this may be seen as a cause for concern by the public but the more recent openness of government and the Citizen's Charter should go some way towards dealing with the matter.

An important example of such rules which are of particular relevance to the built environment is Crichel Down. What are the Crichel Down Rules and how did they evolve?

THE CRICHEL DOWN RULES

Where public authorities have acquired land using their powers of compulsory purchase, they may subsequently find that they need to sell surplus land or it may no longer be required for the purpose for which it was acquired. Principles or rules covering the disposal of such land were established following a major political scandal in 1953 which caused the resignation of the Minister for Agriculture. The controversy of Crichel Down concerned a landowner whose land had been acquired by central government for defence purposes before the war. After this defence use had come to an end, the landowner was not given the opportunity to buy back the land. The Minister for Agriculture in his resignation speech announced new procedures (subsequently to be known as the Crichel Down Rules) for dealing with land acquired 'by compulsion or threat of compulsion' [1].

These principles or rules continue to be applied today and require that 'land should first be offered back to the original owners, at market value, where the land remained in substantially the same state' [1].

Where land is compulsorily acquired by local government, these principles are now contained in the provisions of the legislation including the Local Government Act 1972 and the Acquisition of Land Act 1981. It is therefore evident that in some cases the introduction of administrative rules is subsequently embodied in Civil Service practice.

Green Papers are generally seen to be documents which include rather tentative proposals for discussion and were initially introduced in 1967 by the Labour government. These have in recent years tended to be superseded by Consultation Papers, e.g. Environment Bill: Part III National Parks, January 1995.

GREEN AND WHITE PAPERS

In these cases the government's aim is to gauge reaction to certain policy proposals before making any firm commitment. Responses to such documents are normally made by the various professional bodies, members of the business community, other government departments and public bodies and pressure groups. After due consideration the government produces a firm policy for implementation in the form of a White Paper; Green Papers could therefore be considered to be initial draft White Papers.

White Papers are presented to Parliament by command of Her Majesty and hence are termed as Command Papers and numbered sequentially. At one time White Papers were so called as they were documents in a white cover but today they may vary in colour, size and content. Why should this be the case?

For example, the White Paper of 1986 entitled *Building Businesses not Barriers Cm 9794* ran to eight pages and was merely written text on white paper. The 1994 White Paper *Sustainable Development: The UK Strategy Cm 2426* was more than 265 pages and included a full range of colour and graphics.

Frequently White Papers have at least some elements of policy which will be embodied into subsequent legislation or subordinate legislation. *Building Businesses not Barriers* made some recommendations which were incorporated into the revised Town and Country Planning (Use Classes) Order 1987.

WORKPIECE 6.1

WHITE PAPERS

Identify three White Papers that have been produced during recent years. Discuss how these may influence subsequent legislation.

GUIDANCE DOCUMENTS　How is guidance issued by government and what is its role? Often in order to provide an opportunity for discretion to be used in the implementation of statutory control, central government will offer guidance in various forms in an attempt to influence the decisions of various public authorities. This guidance may be published formally or may be merely advice given through discussion in committee or elsewhere. The vast majority of any ministerial guidance has no statutory basis but some statutes may require 'those to whom guidance is issued' to 'have regard to or take account of the guidance' [2].

For example, the Housing (Homeless Persons) Act 1977 Code of Guidance, 3rd edn 1985, is the current guidance that local authorities shall have regard to in exercising their functions under the Housing Act 1985. But there are likely to be amendments resulting from the White Paper on Housing issued in 1995 which may lead to future legislation and guidance.

Guidance issued by central government is not merely to influence decision makers in government but also provides a useful guide to the development industry, and built environment professionals generally, regarding acceptable courses of action that may arise in certain property development proposals. If one considers land use and planning policy, guidance was previously contained mainly in a range of Circulars (more than 100 by 1988) and a series of Development Control Policy notes. These have been largely superseded by a series of Planning Policy Guidance notes (PPGs), Minerals Policy Guidance Notes and Regional Policy Guidance Notes issued since 1988. Circulars on planning matters now tend to focus on 'the further explanation and elaboration of statutory procedures' [3].

In England and Wales most policy guidance is issued jointly by the DoE and the Welsh Office, except in circumstances where separate advice is necessary. In Scotland the Scottish Office Environment Department (SOEnD) has since 1974 issued a range of national planning guidelines which are currently being replaced with national planning policy guidance.

CIRCULARS　Circulars are published by government departments each year and are an important part of the implementation of central government policy. The most important aspect of circulars to those professionals working in the built environment, whether in the public or private sector, is that many of them give guidance to local authorities as to how legislation should be implemented in practice. Where legislation provides for appeals to a Secretary of State, the criteria contained in Circulars will influence the way the Secretary's appeal decision is reached.

The guidance contained in Circulars has no legal effect *per* se, and local authorities must merely 'have regard' to them in making decisions. Further, Secretaries of State may make decisions which are contrary to their own advice. For example, note the discussion on the SAVE Britain's Heritage case (Chapter 10) where the Secretary of State granted consent to demolish a listed building, overriding his own Circular advice that listed buildings should be retained wherever possible. (This advice is now contained in PPG15.)

Apart from circumstances such as these, the guidance and direction contained in Circulars frequently shape the practices of local authorities implementing built environment law. The courts may accept the importance of these regular practices, and the contents of some Circulars may in effect achieve legal status. In *Coleshill and District Investment Co.* v. *Minister of Housing and Local Government* [4], it was accepted that when a Circular is issued to a local authority it has no legal status, 'but it acquired vitality and strength when, through the years, it passed, as it certainly did, into ... practice' and was acted upon in reaching decisions.

WORKPIECE 6.2

CIRCULARS

Identify three different situations where it has been appropriate for the government to issue a circular. Do you think these forms of guidance play a valuable role today?

Elsewhere in Europe (in the Netherlands, for example) circulars and ministerial notes are used as a guide to the interpretation of the law and if circulars fill a legal void they may become a rule opposable by third parties. White Papers in the Netherlands are called Notas and play an important role in planning law.

PLANNING POLICY GUIDANCE NOTES (PPGs) These documents, issued by the Department of the Environment, were intended to provide information regarding particular policy issues and to minimize the use of the statutory powers available. PPGs are topic based and provide national guidance for certain key land use issues. To date 24 have been issued and are shown in Figure 6.1. These types of document will normally require updating about every five years, perhaps sooner if government legislation requires. PPG1, for example, which was first issued in 1988, outlined the framework for planning and provided a general statement of planning policy but was revised in 1992 to reflect changes introduced by the Town and Country Planning Act 1990 and the Planning and Compensation Act 1991, and to reflect the views of the government White Paper of 1990, *This Common Inheritance.*

PPG number	Title	Year of last revision
1	General Policies and Principles	1992
2	Green Belts	1995
3	Land for Housing	1992
4	Industrial and Commercial Development and Small Firms	1992
5	Simplified Planning Zones	1992
6	Town Centres and Retail Developments	1993
7	Countryside and the Rural Economy	1992
8	Telecommunications	1992
9	Nature Conservation	1994
10	Strategic Guidance for the West Midlands	1988
11	Strategic Guidance for Merseyside	1988
12	Development Plans and Regional Planning Guidance	1992
13	Transport	1994
14	Development on Unstable Land	1990
15	Planning and the Historic Environment	1994
16	Archaeology and Planning	1990
17	Sport and Recreation	1991
18	Enforcing Planning Control	1991
19	Outdoor Advertisement Control	1992
20	Coastal Planning	1992
21	Tourism	1992
22	Renewable Sources of Energy	1993
23	Pollution Control and Waste Management	1994
24	Planning and Noise	1994

Figure 6.1 Status of Planning Policy Guidance notes.

At local level, policy is indicated through Regional Planning Guidance notes (RPGs) and these are area rather than topic based. RPGs are produced by county councils and issued by the DOE, whilst SPGs (Strategic Planning Guidance notes), which apply to metropolitan areas, are produced by central government. An example of the former is RPG 10, *Regional Planning Guidance for the South West* (1995).

Clearly these guidance notes are of great significance to local authority planning departments, developers and built environment professionals as they will be reflected in the form and content of the development plan and also its implementation. Section 54A of the Town and Country Planning Act 1990 [5] states: ' Planning decisions on applications for permission to develop should have regard to the development plan unless material considerations indicate otherwise.' Moore [6] suggests that 'the policy contained in guidance notes constitutes a material consideration'. Paragraph 21 of PPG1 states:

> If decision makers elect not to follow relevant statements of the government's planning policy they must give clear and convincing reasons.

In cases where local authority development plans fail to be consistent with both national and regional guidance, it is likely that, unless there are particular significant local factors that merit such guidance being largely ignored, then these local authorities could find themselves losing planning appeals due to local policy not being in line with government guidance.

Whilst PPGs may set the context for local authority decisions they can, and often do, provide a degree of uncertainty as they may be interpreted in different ways. This uncertainty can effectively be resolved through the appeals process and the courts where appropriate.

NOTES A series of Minerals Policy Guidance notes (13 at the time of writing) and Derelict Land Grant Advice notes (one to date) have also been produced to provide guidance on land use planning matters.

An index of planning guidance is issued periodically by the Department of the Environment which provides an up-to-date document of government guidance available and also includes government publications which promote good practice in development plan preparation and development control business.

WORKPIECE 6.3

CENTRAL GOVERNMENT GUIDANCE

Find two examples of central government guidance relating to the environment. List the main factors included in the guidance.

LOCAL GOVERNMENT POLICY

In addition to policy that is formally conveyed via statutory means (e.g. via the Development Plan), many local authorities may choose to issue informal guidance material. This can come in a variety of forms and might include the production of non-statutory plans, area statements, guidelines for new development, design guides, development and planning briefs and conservation guides. For example, the *Essex Design Guide* produced in 1977 was in fact to be used by many local authorities as the basis for their own policies on new residential development.

WORKPIECE 6.4

LOCAL AUTHORITIES GUIDANCE

Using a local authority area you know well, identify three examples of guidance which are currently in use. Who refers to such guidance? How often is it updated?

POLICY AND JUDGES

Policies proposed and implemented by central and local government, and non-governmental bodies, are often considered by the courts. Such policies are open to the process of judicial review in the High Court where they may be approved or may be declared invalid and quashed. For example, in *Great Portland Estates* v. *Westminster City Council* [7], Great Portland, a major property investor and developer, challenged Westminster's policies on the manner in which it envisaged the future development of the City. The Council proposed that, in future, development would not be allowed if this meant that firms which helped form part of the character of the City (printing, paper, fur, etc.) would be required to leave their premises. As Great Portland Estates owned the freehold in many of the properties within the City, the company was clearly anxious to have such a policy declared invalid. In the House of Lords, Lord Scarman held that this policy of protecting individual occupiers whose activities were traditionally found in certain parts of Westminster was perfectly valid and within the powers of the Council.

Also, judges sometimes adopt their own policy where they believe their decision ought to be made in the public interest. Where these 'policy decisions' are made, judges are sometimes seen as making new law, where Parliament has remained silent on a particular issue. In *Yianni* v. *Edwin Evans* [8], the purchaser of a house sought damages from the surveyor who had carried out a mortgage valuation. The surveyor had declared that the house provided suitable security for a loan to be granted by the building society, but after the purchase had been completed it became apparent that the property had severe structural problems. Prior to this case, the law relating to mortgage valuations was entirely contractual. the surveyor had a contractual relationship with the building society, and the purchaser was not a party to that contract, meaning that he had no redress against the surveyor. The court held that the surveyor owed a duty of care to the purchaser, and even though there was no contract between them, the surveyor knew that the purchaser, in addition to the building society, would rely on that report. In fact, Yianni had not even seen the surveyor's report, which had been forwarded to the building society, but he had relied on the fact that, as a loan was offered to him on the strength of that report, then the house must have been structurally satisfactory; the court held that the surveyor was liable to the purchaser in negligence.

By far the majority of houses sold in the market are 'second-hand' rather than newly built, and until the Yianni decision it is true to say that purchasers of used cars had more legal protection than purchasers of used houses. In one swoop, without the need for Parliamentary intervention in the form of a statute, the court had extended the principles of consumer protection to house purchasers. The decision was followed in numerous later decisions on negligence affecting professionals practising in the built environment and led to the requirement by their professional institutions that all practitioners must be insured against possible negligence claims. They must also continue any professional insurance for a set period of time after they have ceased to practice – a minimum of six years in the case of chartered surveyors.

Whilst the courts may criticize and curb central and local government policies during the process of judicial review, they may also on occasions support the implementation of public policies. One example of such support is the decision in *Bailey* v. *Derby Corporation* [9]. The Corporation was compulsorily acquiring properties for demolition to enable the construction of the Derby ring road. Owners of properties which are expropriated for public schemes are compensated not only for the value of their legal interest in the property taken, but also for the costs of being 'disturbed' in the occupation and enjoyment of their property. A long succession of decisions has resulted in payments such as the costs of finding alternative property, removal costs, interruption of business profits while trade is being built up in the new location, and so on. Bailey, who owned a builder's yard, acted perfectly reasonably and purchased alternative premises in which to relocate his business. However, the long drawn-out process while the road scheme was publicized (confirmed by the Minister of Transport) and the required notices served on owners of properties affected led to stress which caused Mr Bailey to suffer from nervous illness. He therefore claimed not the costs of relocation, as he was too ill to move, but alternatively sought compensation for the closing down of his business.

The prospect that customers will continue to purchase the services or goods of a business is known as the 'goodwill' of the business and when such a business is sold on the open market it has a value which a skilled, experienced surveyor can calculate with reasonable accuracy. The value of goodwill is normally far in excess of the costs incurred in moving the business to another property and hence the decision here was important not merely to Derby Corporation but to all public authorities planning redevelopment schemes. The case was heard at a time when towns and cities in the UK were being reconstructed on a vast scale, at considerable cost to the public purse. Whilst compensation based on the total loss of goodwill, rather than the lower costs of relocation of businesses, would hardly stretch the public purse in the case of one builder in Derby, payments on a similar basis throughout the numerous public development schemes throughout the country clearly would be of concern.

In Bailey's case, there was medical evidence that his health was such that he was unable to tolerate the trauma of moving the business which gave him his livelihood and that he should retire. The Court of Appeal held that the state of health of the claimant, even if it had been caused by the stress of the implementation of the compulsory acquisition, was not the concern of the local authority. Bailey was awarded the costs which would have been incurred had he moved, rather than the value of his business goodwill.

The limitation of the extent of public expenditure is further illustrated in other cases involving public development schemes. In obiter remarks in *Harvey v. Crawley Development Corporation* [10], Lord Denning, MR, thought that while it was reasonable that a dispossessed owner should receive her solicitor's and surveyor's fees incurred in purchasing an alternative property, that principle must not be taken too far: fees (which are normally based on value of the property) must relate to the value of a property similar to the one being compulsorily acquired. Thus, if a better property is purchased, then the fees paid by the acquiring authority must be proportionately reduced – the claimant has received 'value for money' in purchasing a better property and must not be allowed to gain at the public expense.

This 'value for money' concept was developed in later decisions by the courts to the extent that it is now applied if the owner has no choice but to move to more expensive accommodation. For example, the reason many industrial firms occupy outdated workshops in poor repair is because their profit levels do not justify the rent, or purchase price, required to move into more modern premises. On compulsory acquisition of run-down properties to enable a public redevelopment scheme, the occupiers are forced to move, often quickly, and there may be no alternative premises within their price range. If they have no choice other than to take more expensive accommodation, no extra compensation is paid to take account of this: such owners are deemed to have received 'value for money' in their purchase. They were quite content with their original premises, but in the interests of the public purse they are not adequately compensated for a move they did not wish to make.

WORKPIECE 6.5

JUDGES AND INTERPRETATION OF THE LAW

When might a judge, in deciding on a legal dispute, implement a new interpretation of existing law? What circumstances might motivate the judge to do this?

SUMMARY

It is quite clear that whilst government guidance rarely has any statutory basis it can be extremely influential. Hence, decision makers in the built environment frequently incorporate such guidance into policy. Such guidance is subject to consideration by the courts and may in some cases be ignored or overturned. It would, however, be foolhardy to make any development decisions without at least having regard to any guidance material that exists, whether it emanates from central or local government.

This chapter has:

- outlined the range of central government policy documents;
- explained the distinction between Green Papers and White Papers;
- described the role of Circulars, PPGs, MPGs and RPGs in the built environment;

- shown how judges may influence public policy.

CHECKLIST

- Legislation or delegated legislation is normally a reflection of government policy.
- Policy is issued in a variety of ways at both central and local government level.
- Policy may be supported, curbed, criticized or in some cases established by the courts.
- Administrative rules in some cases are subsequently embodied in Civil Service practice.
- Legislation frequently emanates from the publication of Green and White Papers.
- Central government guidance is issued in a wide variety of forms, including Circulars and Planning Policy Guidance, Codes of Practice and Minerals Policy Guidance notes.
- The Welsh and Scottish offices may, where appropriate, issue separate guidance material.
- Consideration of government policies by the courts has had a considerable impact on the role of professionals and development practices within the built environment.

REFERENCES

1. Denyer Green, B. (1994) *Compulsory Purchase and Compensation*, 4th edn, Estates Gazette.
2. DoE/Welsh Office (1992) *Planning Policy Guidance One. General Policy and Principles*, HMSO.
3. Cullingworth, J.B. and Nevin, B. (1994) *Town and Country Planning in Britain*, 11th edn, Routledge.
4. *Coleshill and District Investment Ltd* v. *Ministry of Housing and Local Government* (1969) 1 WLR 746.
5. Town and Country Planning Act 1990, HMSO.
6. Moore, V. (1995) *A Practical Approach to Planning Law*, 5th edn, Blackstone Press.
7. *Westminster CC* v. *Great Portland Estates Plc* (1985) AC 661.
8. *Yianni* v. *Edwin Evans & Sons* (1982) QB 438.
9. *Bailey* v. *Derby Corporation* (1965) 1 AL ER 443.
10. *Harvey* v. *Crawley Development Corporation* (1957) 1 QB 485.

FURTHER READING

Cairns, W. and McKeon, R. (1995) *Introduction to French Law*, Cavendish.
Shaw, J. (ed) (1993) *European Community Law*, Macmillan.
Wade, H.W.R. and Forsyth, C.F. (1994) *Administrative Law*, 7th edn, Clarendon Press, Oxford.

ELEMENTS OF THE
LAW IN PRACTICE

**PART
TWO**

PRIVATE LAW: CONTRACT

HELEN SMITHEMAN

What is a contract? Most people would understand it to be a legal agreement. Many probably think that it is a formal written document which applies only to specific types of legal relationships, but they would be surprised to learn that everyone makes contracts every day of their lives. When you buy a newspaper, take a train ride or go to the hairdresser, those transactions are governed by the same rules as the complex multi-page negotiations entered into by big business.

This chapter examines the basic framework of the law of contract its role in the built environment.

After reading this chapter you should be able to:

● understand the role and functions of contract law in modern society;

● comprehend the nature of a contract through its various stages of formation, vitiating factors and discharge;

● identify the component aspects of a valid contract;

● indicate in which situations an agreement will not be upheld by the courts;

● describe the several forms of discharge and use of contractual remedies.

Once society starts to operate on the basis of exchange of goods and services, then that process must be regulated by rules in order for it to function efficiently. Most of the law of contract developed in the nineteenth century during the Industrial Revolution. The rules were evolved through the courts rather than by legislative intervention. Unlike some areas of law, the contract is a transaction entered into on a voluntary basis. No one is forced to become a party to a contract. As such, in the nineteenth century the judges took the view that if the agreement was entered into freely then they would not interfere with its terms. This was known as the concept of *laissez-faire* (freedom to make the contract of their choice). That doctrine works efficiently where the parties are of 'equal bargaining power' and can both determine the terms of the contract. However, where one party is economically stronger and can impose terms on the weaker party the concept becomes unjust. Today the law through legislation is far more paternalistic and insists on the inclusion of certain terms. This can be found in employment contracts, sales of goods and services, housing agreements and the like.

VIEWS ON THE FUNCTIONS OF CONTRACT

Whilst contracts are used regularly by the commercial world, these agreements are approached differently by different people. The lawyer will look at the structure of the agreement to see if it is valid and will wish to ascertain whether the elements of formation of a valid contract are present.

On the other hand, the business person sees a contract as an instrument of commercial planning, a document or series of documents which make arrangements for important and often complicated commercial matters, such as delivery of materials, testing and approval of equipment, certification and payments, dealings with subcontractors and suppliers and industrial and intellectual property rights [1].

Those matters would be of little interest to the lawyer if the form of the agreement was not a legally enforceable document. The courts will grant a remedy to a party suffering loss only if the loss arose from a valid, enforceable contract.

The importance of ensuring that the negotiations are conducted within the framework of what the court will recognize as a contract is illustrated in the case of *British Steel Corporation* v. *Cleveland Bridge and Engineering* Co. *Ltd* (1984) [2], where the parties had entered into contractual negotiations for the production of cast steel nodes for a building project. The work was started without a formal contract being issued, although terms were discussed. There was late delivery and court proceedings resulted. Despite the fact that most of the work had been done, the court refused to recognize the existence of a contract and the only court order was for a reasonable price for the stock delivered [1].

The law of contract is vast and can often be somewhat confusing to the uninformed. This chapter aims to provide a brief outline of contract law. Further detail can be found in specialist contract texts.

Contract can be divided into three main subject areas:

- First, there is **formation of the contract**, which traditionally meant that the court had to be satisfied that all the elements were present before it would hold that a contract existed. Courts today may be more flexible in their approach.
- The second stage is **vitiating factors**. There may appear to be a validly formed contract but it becomes obvious that something went wrong in the formation stage and the apparently valid contract can be avoided.
- Finally there are **discharge** and **remedies**. This involves the termination of a contract.

All contracts are agreements, but not all agreement are contracts.

- There must be a valid **offer** which has been **accepted** and supported by valid **consideration**.
- The parties must **intend** the agreement to be legally binding.
- The agreement must be entered into with **consent**.
- The parties must have legal **capacity to contract**.
- The contract must be **lawful**.

In English law it has become obligatory to regard an agreement as consisting of offer and acceptance. What do these terms mean?

There must be at least two parties to a contract. The person making the offer is usually referred to as the **offerer**. The recipient of the offer is the **offeree**, and when the offer is accepted that person becomes the **acceptor**. There are various rules relating to offer and acceptance. Lawyers speak of offer and acceptance but in a commercial environment there may be a certain chain of communications: Table 7.1 gives an example.

In commercial contracts, the most frequent offers are tenders and quotations made by sellers or contractors and purchase orders made by prospective customers. Some quotations and estimates may not be offers according to their wording. In *Crowshaw* v. *Pritchard and Renwich* (1899) [3], it was held that an estimate could amount to an offer and there was no fixed rule that the estimate could not be an offer. A building contract which exists between a contractor or builder and an employer or building owner is still judged by the principles of the law of contract, despite its

STRUCTURE OF A CONTRACT

FORMATION OF THE CONTRACT: OFFER AND ACCEPTANCE

OFFER

complexity. Building works have generally been subject to control under 'JCT contracts' (issued by the Joint Contracts Tribunal). More recently, the New Engineering Contract has been introduced as a replacement.

Table 7.1 Chain of communication

Step	Communication	Sent by
1.	The invitation to tender	Purchaser
2.	The tender or quotation	Seller
3.	Acknowledgement of the tender	Purchaser
4.	Letter of intent	Purchaser
5.	Acknowledgement of letter of intent	Seller
6.	Formal order based on the tender	Purchaser
7.	Acknowledgement of the order	Seller

Contract law lecturers enjoy setting examination questions or coursework in which the students have to plough their way through various steps of negotiations to decide whether there is a contract or not. If you enjoy problem solving it is quite a satisfying exercise, and requires the application of the basic principles of contract law to each aspect of the question asked by the lecturer.

The offer must be firm, certain and communicated to the offeree. This means that the offerer must intend the proposal to be an offer, that the terms of the proposal are clear and that the offeree is made aware of the offer. The requirement that the offer is firm relates to the party's intention when making the statement. Sometimes the court holds that a preliminary statement is not an offer. What type of statement is not on offer?

STATEMENT OF PRICE   A mere indication by the owner of a sale price does not amount to an offer; see *Harvey* v. *Facey* (1893) [4].

THE GIVING OF INFORMATION   The communication of information is not an offer or acceptance. Examples may be a catalogue, price list or factual answer to a question about particular types of goods. In these cases the court will normally find that rather than making an offer there has been an 'invitation to treat' (it is then up to a potential purchaser to make an offer).

INVITATION TO TREAT Normally there is an offer and an acceptance. However, in some circumstances the offer may be seen as merely an opportunity to bargain. This term in law is known as an invitation to treat. This is an indication by one party that he wishes to enter into contractual negotiations but the statement made does not incur any legal liability. There must then be an offer and an acceptance for a contractual relationship to arise.

Invitations to treat are used in the following situations:

● Display of goods in shops.
● Advertisements for sale of goods and services (e.g houses for sale in estate agents' offices); see *Pharmaceutical Society of Great Britain* v. *Boots Cash Chemists Ltd* (1953) [5].
● Auctions (e.g land and property); see *Payne* v. *Cave* (1789) [6].
● Tenders (e.g development contracts); see *Harvela Investments Ltd* v. *Royal Trust Co. of Canada (CI) Ltd* (1985) [7].

WORKPIECE 7.1

OFFER AND ACCEPTANCE

Using the table below, indicate the contractual stages of the following situations:

Situation	Invitation to treat	Offer	Acceptance
Display of goods in shop			
Auction			
Advertisement for sale of goods			
Tender			

The requirement for certainty relates to the terms of the offer. If they are not clear then the court may refuse to recognize the statement as an offer. For instance sale of a car 'on the usual hire purchase terms' is too vague.

The last element is that of communication. An offer can be made to an individual, a group or the whole world. In the case of *Carlill* v. *Carbolic Smokeball Co.* (1891–4) [8] the court held that an offer could be made to the public at large. (This case is well worth reading. It involves an amusing situation and very determined defence lawyers who ran a number of defences to the claim, so that the case illustrates a number of legal points.)

ACCEPTANCE

The response by the offeree must be an unqualified assent to the terms of the offer and must normally be communicated to the offerer.

COUNTER OFFERS   As with offers, there are statements which the courts have held would not be valid acceptance. If the offeree inserts new terms then it is a counter offer which destroys the original offer, and the counter offer must itself be accepted before there is a valid contract; *Hyde* v. *Wrench* (1840) [9].

This must be distinguished from a request for information where the offeree is simply asking for clarification of the terms and the original offer remains open; *Stevenson, Jaques & Co.* v. *McLean* (1880) [10].

COMMUNICATION   The acceptance must be communicated to the offerer and received by him before the acceptance is effective. The offerer cannot impose silence as a means of acceptance; *Felthouse* v. *Bindley* (1862) [11].

There are two exceptions to the rule on communication. If the offer is unilateral then the offeree does not have to communicate acceptance. A unilateral offer is one which requires the offeree to carry out an act, e.g. 'the first person to swim the Channel wins £100'. The offer is accepted by performing the act; *Carlill* v. *Carbolic Smokeball Co.* [8].

THE POSTAL RULE   The other exception is use of the postal rule. If the post is an appropriate means of acceptance then the acceptance is valid as soon as the acceptance is posted; *Adams* v. *Lindsell* (1818) [12].

The letter must be correctly addressed and posted and will create a binding contract even if the offerer never receives the letter. In cases where fax or e-mail is used as a way of conveying an offer, the contract is made when the acceptance is received by the offerer.

TERMINATION OF OFFER   Once an offer has been made how can it be terminated? This can occur in various ways:

- by accepting an offer, a binding contract is made and the offer lapses;
- by rejection: the offeree is not bound to accept the offer;
- by revocation: provided that the offeree receives the revocation before an effective acceptance has been made, then the offer ends;
- by lapse of time;
- by death of the offerer;
- by death of the offeree.

AGREEMENT

'For sale, complete set of Snow White models in plastic, each figure two feet high, weather and frost resistant. Twelve figures in all, £24. Phone Newport 0001 or write to Lucas, The Grotto, Magnolia Gardens, Newport.'

1. On Sunday, Angela wrote enclosing a cheque for £24 and saying: 'If I do not hear anything by Thursday I will assume the dear little things are mine.'

2. On Monday, Bertha wrote saying: 'I offer you £20 for the lot.' This arrived on Tuesday and Lucas wrote back saying: 'No, I want £30.' When Bertha received this, she sent a letter saying: 'Yes I accept and enclose £5 and will pay the remainder off at £5 a month.'

3. Meanwhile, Cynthia wrote on Wednesday saying: 'I will buy the gnomes for £24.' Lucas replied, saying: 'I want £30.' His letter was posted on Thursday. Cynthia received it on Saturday, when she posted a reply saying: 'I accept.'

4. Meanwhile Lucas had written to Cynthia on Friday saying: 'Sorry, I have decided to keep them.' Cynthia received this letter on the following Monday.

5. It is now Tuesday of the following week and Angela, Bertha and Cynthia have all arrived on Lucas's doorstep.

Get together in a group, discuss these facts and then briefly advise Lucas of his legal position.

INTENTION TO CREATE LEGAL RELATIONS

This aspect of formation of a contract looks at whether the parties intended the contract to be legally binding. For these purposes agreements are divided into two types: commercial and domestic.

COMMERCIAL AGREEMENTS   Here the court presumes that the parties intended the agreement to be a contract and no proof need be brought. In fact it is the party who wishes to allege that the agreement is not a contract who must bring the proof that the agreement was not intended to be a contract. This is usually done via wording in the agreement, e.g. *Jones* v. *Vernons Pools* (1938) [13].

This point is relevant to building contracts where the main contractor employs a subcontractor using a 'letter of intent'. The contract with the subcontractor will be effective only if the main contractor is awarded the contract by his client.

DOMESTIC AGREEMENTS   Here the court presumes that informal agreements made between friends or members of the same family are not contracts. It is for the person who wishes to prove that the agreement is a contract to bring the appropriate evidence. Particularly in the case of agreements between spouses, the courts have developed a set of rules to deal with these disputes; see *Balfour* v. *Balfour* (1919) [14] and *Merritt* v. *Merritt* (1970) [15].

CONSIDERATION

The last element of formation of a contract is the necessity for consideration. This turns an agreement into a binding contract. The law requires that both parties contribute to the agreement for it to be legally binding. Consideration can be 'executory', which is a promise in return for a promise, or 'executed', which is an act in return for a promise. In order for an act to be valid consideration it must be legally 'sufficient' but this does not mean commercially adequate.

SUFFICIENCY   If the promisee (the party to whom the promise has been made) is already obliged to do that task then a promise to pay them for doing it cannot be enforced. In *Collins* v. *Godefroy* (1831) [16], the plaintiff was promised a fee if he gave evidence at court. In fact he had already been summonsed to give evidence; he was obliged to attend and had not done anything over and above what he was already bound to do. However, when the promisee does something extra then the payment may be upheld; *Glasbrook Bros Ltd* v. *Glamorgan County Council* (1925) [17].

Using the same principle in contract, if the promisee is simply carrying out the terms of the contract the offer of extra payment is not valid; *Stilk* v. *Myrick* (1809) [18]. Equally, requiring the promisee to do substantially more than his contractual duty may allow payment.

This original rule has been slightly changed by the case of *Williams* v. *Roffey Bros & Nicholls (Contractors) Ltd* (1990) [19], where the promisor obtained benefit by getting the promisee to carry out performance of the contract (the promisee did not have to pay a penalty for late completion). However, the courts have since then indicated that this rule appears to be limited to the facts in Williams. Other examples of sufficient consideration include agreeing not to sue if the promisor settles the claim; *Alliance Bank* v. *Broom* (1864) [20].

Also, where the promisor agrees to do something for a second party but is already bound by contract to do this for a third party, then it is valid consideration; *Scotson* v. *Pegg* (1861) [21].

ADEQUACY   On the other hand, the court does not require that the exchange is of equal value, provided that something is exchanged; *Chappell & Co. Ltd* v. *Nestle Co. Ltd* (1960) [22].

PAST CONSIDERATION   It is important that the promise comes before the act. If someone acts and is then promised payment, there is no consideration for that promise and the claim will fail; *Re McArdle* 1951.

RELATIONS

Decide which of the items listed below relate to the areas above.

domestic agreement
Merritt v. *Merritt*
repudiation before 18 years
Collin v. *Godefroy*
legal sufficiency
sane, sober and 18 or over
beneficial contract for service
loans
Balfour v. *Balfour*
executory
partnership agreements
Re McArdle
necessary goods
extra act carried out

Chappell & Co
adult guarantee of loan
executed
contracts of permanent nature
Jones v. *Vernons Pools*
contractual duty
drink persons contract
agreements between spouses
Scotson v. *Peggy*
not paid out of general assets
past act
purchase of shares
contracts of training
informal agreements
unnecessary goods
commercial agreement
Glasbrook Bros, Glamorgan
notification after 18 years

FORM OF THE CONTRACT

Contracts may be written or verbal, but there are some contracts which must be by deed (transfer of land and assignment of lease for three years). Some contracts must be written, and these include contracts for the sale of land and consumer credit agreements. Also some contracts must be evidenced in writing, such as contracts of guarantee.

CONTENTS OF A CONTRACT

Once the court is satisfied that there is a contract, it must establish the terms of the contract (Figure 7.1). This will indicate the obligations imposed on each party to the contract. This is particularly important where the negotiations have been prolonged and the contents of the contract are complicated. Not all of the negotiations may become terms of the contract, and not all of the terms may have been written down or even discussed by the parties. The terms have to be divided into major and minor terms. Sometimes parties may be able to exclude or limit their liability and these appear as 'exemption clauses'.

(a)

Representations	Terms
1) Maker of statement asks other party to check truth	Maker of statement tries to stop other party checking truth
	2) Statement so important person would not have made contract without it *Bannernman* v. *White* 1861
	3) Maker of statement has special expertise to establish truth of statement *Dick Bentley* v. *Harold Smith* 1965
4) Timing of statement – if there was long gap between statement and making of contract *Routledge* v. *McKay* 1954	

(b)

Express terms	Implied terms
Those terms which are articulated between the parties and are either written or verbal	Those terms not specifically mentioned but treated as part of the contract
	Implied by custom – local/trade custom *Hutton* v. *Warren* 1836
	Implied by statute – Sale of Goods Act 1979 – Supply of Goods and Services Act 1982
	Implied by the courts – used to determine intention of the parties Two tests: 1) Business efficacy – term needed to make a contract viable The Moorcock 1889 2) Officious bystander test – If such a person suggested the term the parties would respond 'Oh yes but of course' *Wilson* v. *Best Travel* 1993

(c) Importance of terms

Conditions	Warranties
Major term which goes to the root of the contract *Poussard* v. *Spiers & Pond* 1876	Minor term which if breached causes some loss but does not affect main purpose of contract

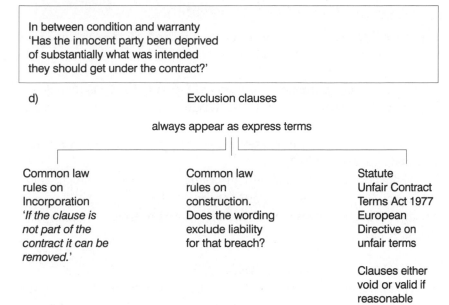

Intermediate terms

In between condition and warranty
'Has the innocent party been deprived
of substantially what was intended
they should get under the contract?'

d)   Exclusion clauses

always appear as express terms

| Common law rules on Incorporation *'If the clause is not part of the contract it can be removed.'* | Common law rules on construction. Does the wording exclude liability for that breach? | Statute Unfair Contract Terms Act 1977 European Directive on unfair terms

Clauses either void or valid if reasonable |

Figure 7.1 Terms of a contract.

VITIATING FACTORS

The second main area of the form and function of a contract concerns vitiating factors, otherwise known as 'policing the bargain'. Sometimes a contract appears to be validly formed, containing agreement, consideration and contractual intention. If a vitiating element is present then the courts may choose not to enforce the contract. The vitiating factors which may have a policing role include capacity, duress, undue influence, illegality, mistake and misrepresentation. If such a vitiating factor is present, the court will hold that the contract is contravened, and this has one of five consequences:

● The contract made is void (the contract is treated as if it had never existed and the parties have no rights at all).
● The contract is avoidable (the contract is valid unless or until the injured party avoids it).
● The contract is unenforceable by either party (the contract is valid but neither party can sue for breach).
● The contract is unenforceable by one party (the contract cannot be enforced against a member of a particular group, e.g. minors, but can be enforced against the other person).

● The contract is enforceable with changes (the contract continues to exist but the court alters the terms).

It is beyond the scope of this chapter to go through all the rules in detail but the areas will be explained briefly.

CAPACITY

The law recognizes the need to protect certain individuals if they are incapable through age or mental impairment. The usual rule is that you must be sane, sober and at least 18 years of age to enter into a valid contract. Therefore the law protects the mentally disordered, drunken persons and children.

Contracts made by mentally disordered or drunk people are voidable because they did not give real consent to the agreement. When the person is sober or regains mental capacity they may agree to be bound by the contract.

CONTRACTS MADE BY MINORS   The law has to balance the need to protect minors against unscrupulous influence by adults to enter into unsuitable contracts, against the right of the adult trader to be paid for the items transferred under the contract. The usual rule is that for necessary goods/services the minor must pay a reasonable price for the items. If the goods are luxuries the minor must either return them or refund the proceeds of sale of any items. If the goods have been consumed then minors are not expected to pay out of their general assets and the adults must bear the loss. The types of minors' contracts are detailed in Figure 7.2.

CONSENT

In order for the contract to be valid it must be entered into freely and voluntarily. The following factors cover agreements where the consent is invalidated in some way.

DURESS   Here the person agreed to the contract only because they were threatened in some way. There may be actual physical violence or threat of violence; for example, *Barton* v. *Armstrong* (1976) [23]. Economic duress causing financial loss is recognized by the court as sufficient to make the contract voidable; *Atlas Express Ltd* v. *Kafco (Importers and Distributors) Ltd* (1989) [24].

UNDUE INFLUENCE   This occurs where one party uses their influence to take unfair advantage of the other person. The various positions of undue influence are shown in Figure 7.3.

Type	Description
Valid	Contracts for necessary goods/services Contracts for beneficial contracts of training, education
Effect	Minor is bound by contract and must pay reasonable price

Voidable	Contracts of a permanent nature, e.g.:
	    purchase of shares
	    interest in land
	    partnership agreements

Effect	Minor is bound unless he repudiates contract which must be done before he is 18 or within a reasonable time of reaching 18
Unenforceable	Contracts for unnecessary goods, loans
Effect	Minor not bound unless he notifies after reaching 18. Minor's Contracts Act 1987 makes adult guarantee of loan to minor enforceable

Figure 7.2 Types of contract for minors.

The effect of some mistakes is to make the contract void. However, not every mistake will operate to void the contract. The usual rule is that of *caveat emptor* – 'let the buyer beware'. This means that it is the responsibility of buyers to check what they are buying. If they make a mistake as to the quality of the item then the contract is not vitiated. The courts recognize only a limited number of mistakes as being operative to avoid the contract:

MISTAKE

● In **common mistake** the offer and acceptance correspond but the parties make the same mistake.
● In **mutual mistake** both parties make a mistake, but it is not the same mistake and therefore there is no agreement between the parties.
● In **unilateral mistake** only one party makes mistake, but the other party knows of the mistake and does not correct it.

Examples of common mistake include where the subject matter of the contract does not exist at the time the contract was made: *Couturier* v. *Hastie* (1856) [25]; *Wood* v. *Scarth* (1858) [26].

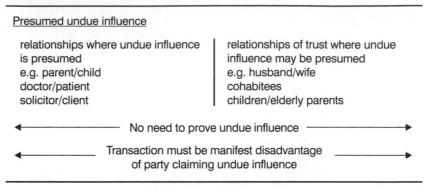

Actual undue influence

This must be proved *Williams* v *Bayley* 1866.
Since 1993 (*CIBC Mortgages plc* v *Pitt*) no need to show agreement was to manifest disadvantage of plaintiff.

Presumed undue influence

| relationships where undue influence is presumed e.g. parent/child doctor/patient solicitor/client | relationships of trust where undue influence may be presumed e.g. husband/wife cohabitees children/elderly parents |

←——————— No need to prove undue influence ———————→

←——— Transaction must be manifest disadvantage ———→
of party claiming undue influence

Special situation of three-party transaction
Barclays Bank v *O'Brien* 1993
CIBC Mortgages plc v *Pitt* 1993

Figure 7.3 Undue influence.

Unilateral mistake includes **mistake of intention** – if one party makes a mistake about their intention and the other party knew or ought to have known of the mistake, the contract will be void: *Hartog* v. *Colin and Shields* (1939) [27].

Mistake of identity is the most common use of unilateral mistake. Such mistakes are nearly always provoked by the conduct of the other party which amounts to a fraudulent misrepresentation. The difficulty is that misrepresentation makes the contract **voidable**, not void. In such cases the property may be acquired and then sold to a third person. The 'rogue' disappears, leaving the original owner to try to recover the property from the third person. If the mistake as to identity is operative then the contract is **void**: ownership of the goods did not pass and the third person must return the goods. The rules on mistaken identity are explained in Figure 7.4.

ILLEGALITY

If a contract is illegal in any way, the courts will not enforce it. This is for reasons of public policy. Sometimes the courts will interfere with the terms of a contract to protect a public interest which is more important than the interest of the parties (for example, price fixing by large companies). The second aspect of public policy concerns contracts which are unfair between the parties. The law on illegality is complex and

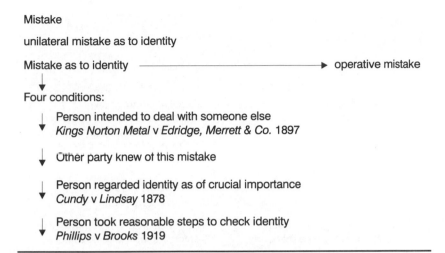

Mistake

unilateral mistake as to identity

Mistake as to identity ——————————————————→ operative mistake
↓
Four conditions:

↓ Person intended to deal with someone else
▼ *Kings Norton Metal* v *Edridge, Merrett & Co.* 1897

↓ Other party knew of this mistake

↓ Person regarded identity as of crucial importance
▼ *Cundy* v *Lindsay* 1878

↓ Person took reasonable steps to check identity
▼ *Phillips* v *Brooks* 1919

Figure 7.4 Mistakes.

detailed. For ease of understanding at this stage illegal contracts have been divided into various categories, referred to in Figure 7.5.

The last vitiating factor links up with representations, as referred to earlier. Where one party makes a statement which is not incorporated into the contract but influences the making of the contract and is wrong, the party suffering loss cannot sue in breach of contract because the statement is not part of the contract. Therefore the law has developed the rule of misrepresentation to cover such situations. A misrepresentation is an untrue statement of fact which induces the other party to enter the contract. The party suffering loss must establish the type of misrepresentation made, as that will affect the remedy sought.

There are three types of misrepresentation:

- **Fraudulent**. The person making the statement knew or was reckless as to the truth of the statement.
- **Negligent**. The person could have made reasonable efforts to establish the truth of the statement, but essentially the statement was made innocently without any dishonesty.
- **Innocent**. The false statement was made and the maker could not have known that the statement was false.

The position on remedies for these situations is described in Figure 7.6.

MISREPRESENTATION

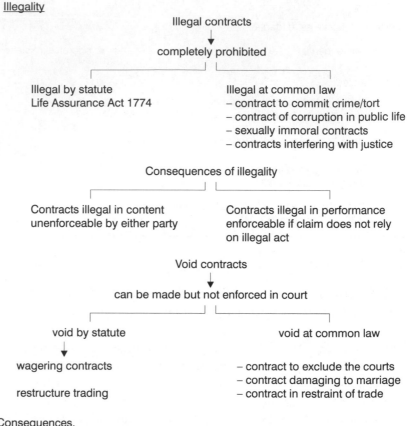

Illegality

Illegal contracts
↓
completely prohibited

Illegal by statute
Life Assurance Act 1774

Illegal at common law
– contract to commit crime/tort
– contract of corruption in public life
– sexually immoral contracts
– contracts interfering with justice

Consequences of illegality

Contracts illegal in content
unenforceable by either party

Contracts illegal in performance
enforceable if claim does not rely
on illegal act

Void contracts
↓
can be made but not enforced in court

void by statute
↓
wagering contracts

restructure trading

void at common law

– contract to exclude the courts
– contract damaging to marriage
– contract in restraint of trade

Consequences.
– any money paid may be recovered
– if only part of contract is void possible to sever this part leaving remainder valid
  Court must be able to act out void part (blue penal test) to leave the rest to
  make sense

Figure 7.5 Illegality.

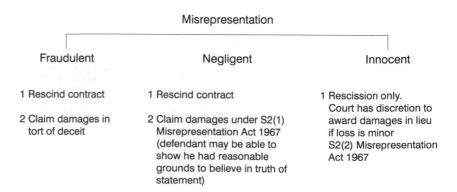

Misrepresentation

Fraudulent	Negligent	Innocent
1 Rescind contract	1 Rescind contract	1 Rescission only. Court has discretion to award damages in lieu if loss is minor S2(2) Misrepresentation Act 1967
2 Claim damages in tort of deceit	2 Claim damages under S2(1) Misrepresentation Act 1967 (defendant may be able to show he had reasonable grounds to believe in truth of statement)	

Figure 7.6 Misrepresentation.

CASE STUDIES ON VITIATING FACTORS

1. Percy was induced to buy a lorry from Dennis after hearing representations as to its condition and a statement that it would do 11 miles to the gallon. Shortly after buying the lorry Percy discovered that it had several serious defects and the petrol consumption was 5 miles to the gallon. Advise Percy.

2. Norman answered an advertisement to purchase a second-hand Rolls Royce from Norma. They agreed a price and Norma indicated she wished to be paid in cash. Norman said he preferred to pay by cheque and produced a business card. He had stolen this card from the local MP. Norma checked the details in the phone book and agreed to take the cheque. Norman drove off in the car and promptly sold it to Gloria. His cheque bounced. Norma sued Gloria for the return of the car. Advise them both as to their legal rights.

3. Robert Banks and Nick Quick decided to burgle houses together and split the proceeds equally. Nick took the goods and sold them to a fence. He then refused to give the money to Robert. Can Robert sue Nick?

TERMINATION OF THE CONTRACT

The final area for discussion regarding contract relates to discharge. How can a contract be discharged, or terminated?

There are four methods of terminating the contract: by performance, by agreement, by frustration or by breach.

BY PERFORMANCE   The usual rule is that the contract must be performed completely and precisely by both parties; *Cutter* v. *Powell* (1795) [28].

However, there are a number of exceptions to this rule (Figure 7.7).

BY AGREEMENT   Once an agreement has been made the parties can agree to end it. If neither party has performed their part then the consideration for the new contract is the promise not to enforce the original obligation. If one party has performed their part and agrees to release the other party from their part, then the latter must provide consideration for that promise.

BY FRUSTRATION   This doctrine goes against the performance rule. Under the rule of performance, if one party cannot perform their part then they are in breach. This would apply even if through changed circumstances, not of their making, the contract was impossible to perform; *Davis Contractors Ltd* v. *Fareham UDC* (1956) [29]. However, the law has developed various categories of frustration (Figure 7.8).

Performance must be precise and exact

Defective performance = no payment

Exceptions	Description
severable obligations	Contract broken into independent parts so payment enforced for each
preventing performance	Performer prevented from completing is entitled to payment for work done *Planche* v *Colburn* 1831
accepting part performance	Accepting party must have real choice in accepting *Sumpter* v *Hedges* 1898
substantial performance	Provided majority of work done, performer entitled to payment. If failed part relates to a condition then it cannot be claimed. *Bolton* v *Mahadeva* 1972

Figure 7.7 Performance.

BY BREACH   A party who fails to perform, or performs defectively, is in breach of contract. The remedy for the injured party will depend on the term breached (Figure 7.9).

REMEDIES FOR BREACH OF CONTRACT

A number of remedies for breach of contract are provided by the law but they are not always very effective. It is much more appropriate to consider possible solutions prior to any breaches arising. The standard form of building contract, for example, includes various contingencies, which alleviates the need to go to court. This should enable the parties to keep on good business terms. Examples of some remedies are shown in Figure 7.10.

SUMMARY

Contracts are seen as a type of bargain. Both (all) parties must make a contribution to such a bargain. A contract may be defined as an agreement which is binding on the parties. Whilst no complete set of rules exists for the making of a contract there are clearly defined legal guidelines that are usually applied. There can be no doubt that contracts are a very important aspect of life in the modern world and an understanding of their role is essential.

DISCHARGE

Sidney owns a company which specializes in providing automatic catering facilities for building firms. He enters into a contract with a large firm to provide catering on three sites. It is arranged to transport the equipment on a Sunday when the sites are quiet.

Explain the legal position in each of the following situations:

● The bridge over the river is closed because of high wind and the alternative route adds 50 miles to the journey.

● To reduce petrol consumption a law is passed banning business traffic on Sundays.

● Sidney contracts with another firm for the same day. His van fails its MOT on Friday and Sidney decides to carry out the second contract.

● Sidney and his employees became ill with 'flu and cannot leave their beds on Sunday.

● Sidney completes the work save for one unit which cannot fit in the van. He refuses to make a second journey to complete the contract.

Category	Description
supervening illegality	After contract made, law passed making performance illegal *Denny Mott Dickson* v *James Fraser* 1944
destruction of subject matter	After contract made subject matter ceases to exist *Taylor* v *Caldwell* 1863
unavailability of party	Personal contract and person ill/unavailable for period of time *Morgan* v *Manser* 1948; *Hare* v *Murphy Bros* 1974
fundamental purpose	If performance is radically different to original purpose then contract is frustrated *Krell* v *Henry* 1903; *Herne Bay* v *Hutton* 1903
performance more expensive/ difficult to carry out	Unless contract specifies for this such situations do not amount to frustration *Davis Contractors* v *Fareham DC* 1956

> ### Effects of Frustration
> Law Reform (Frustrated Contracts) Act 1943
> – money paid before frustration can be recovered
> – money payable before frustration no longer preferable
> – expenses incurred before frustration can be claimed
> – valuable benefit given before frustration can be claimed

Figure 7.8 Frustration.

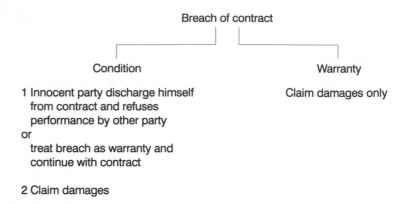

Figure 7.9 Breach of contract.

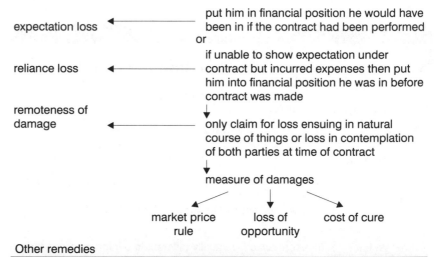

Figure 7.10 Remedies for breach of contract.

This chapter has:

- explored the function and nature of contracts;
- investigated the legal rules necessary for the formation of a valid contract;
- examined the situation when the court will not enforce a contract;
- looked at the different types of discharge.

- The role and function of contract law is to regulate business agreements and to give remedies in the event of breach of contract.
- The traditional perception of contract requires that the agreement should contain certain component parts such as offer, acceptance, consideration and intention to create legal relations.
- The existence of certain factors such as mistake, misrepresentation, duress, undue influence and illegality will affect the validity of the contract.
- There is a necessity to provide remedies for discharge of the contract through defective performance, breach and frustration.

1. Galbraith, A. and Stockdale, M. (1993) *Building and Land Management Law for Students*, 3rd edn, Newnes.
2. [1984] 1ALL ER 504.
3. *Crowshaw* v. *Pritchard and Renwich* (1899).
4. *Harvey* v. *Facey* (1893) AC 552.
5. *Pharmaceutical Society of Great Britain* v. *Boots Cash Chemists Ltd* (1953) 1QB 401.
6. *Payne* v. *Cave* (1789) 100 ER 502.
7. *Harvela Investments Ltd* v. *Royal Trust Co. of Canada* (1985) 2 All ER 127.
8. *Carlill* v. *Carbolic Smokeball Co.* (1891–4) All ER Rep 127.
9. *Hyde* v. *Wrench* (1840) 49 ER 132.
10. *Stevenson, Jaques & Co.* v. *McLean* (1880) 55 QBD 346.
11. *Felthouse* v. *Bindley* (1862) 142 ER 1037.
12. *Adams* v. *Lindsell* (1818) IB & Ald. 681.
13. *Jones* v. *Vernons Pools* (1938) 2 All ER 626.
14. *Balfour* v. *Balfour* (1919) 2KB 571.
15. *Merritt* v. *Merritt* (1970) 1 WLR 1211.
16. *Collins* v. *Godefroy* (1831) 1B & Ad 950.
17. *Glasbrook Bros Ltd* v. *Glamorgan County Council* (1925) AC 270.
18. *Stilk* v. *Myrick* (1809) 170 ER 626.
19. *Williams* v. *Roffey Bros & Nicholls (Contractors) Ltd* (1990) 1 All ER 1168.
20. *Alliance Bank* v. *Broom* (1864) 62 ER 631.
21. *Scotson* v. *Pegg* (1861) 3 LT 753.

22.   *Chappell & Co. Ltd* v. *Nestle Co. Ltd* (1960) AC 87.
23.   *Barton* v. *Armstrong* (1976) AC 104.
24.   *Atlas Express Ltd* v. *Kafco (Importers and Distributors) Ltd* (1989) 1 All ER.
25.   *Couturier* v. *Hastie* (1856) 5HL 673.
26.   *Wood* v. *Scarth* (1858) 1 F&F 293.
27.   *Hartog* v. *Colin and Shields* (1939) 3 All ER 566.
28.   *Cutter* v. *Powell* (1975) 6TR 320.
29.   *Davis Contractors Ltd* v. *Fareham UDC* (1956) AC 666.

FURTHER READING

Adams, J.N. and Brownsward, R. (1995) *Key Issues in Contract Law*, Butterworths.

Clough, R. (1994) *Construction Contracting*. Wiley.

Horn, N., Kotz, H. and Leser, H. (1982) *German Private and Commercial Law*, Clarendon.

PRIVATE LAW: TORT

PETER BARRETT AND RICHARD JORDAN

This chapter deals with the way in which the law seeks to strike a balance between conflicting interests in society. The later part of the chapter particularly deals with the control of rights and obligations stemming from the use and occupation of land.

THEME

After reading this chapter you should be able to:

OBJECTIVES

● understand the basic principles involved in ensuring that individuals are held accountable for their acts or ommissions;

● be aware of the responsiblities that individuals have in terms of the way they use land and buildings;

● identify potential areas of conflict and how the law is used to resolve them.

In order to achieve a balance between conflicting interests in society, the law confers certain rights on individuals but also imposes obligations on them. The law of tort is concerned with the legal relationship between individuals which arises as a direct result of their reliance upon these legal rights and obligations. The term 'tort' is French in origin and means a wrong.

INTRODUCTION

Where the balance is upset following some unlawful and/or unreasonable act, or omission to act, by one party (the **defendant**) which causes direct and foreseeable harm to another (the **plaintiff**) the law of tort steps in to act as a loss adjuster. The wrong-doer is required to make amends, often in the form of monetary compensation, or **damages**, being paid to the injured party. There are numerous torts identifiable whereby the behaviour of one party causes or threatens to cause harm to another. These include the tort of negligence, the tort of trespass and the tort of nuisance. Much of the law relating to tort has developed through court decisions and some rules have been incorporated into legislation, e.g. Occupiers Liability Act 1984.

NEGLIGENCE

Negligence as a legal concept is a particular branch of the law of tort which has a specific meaning. It is not merely concerned with carelessness or neglect in the ordinary sense of the word. Rather, it is the failure on the part of the defendant to take such care as the law requires to ensure that no harm comes to the plaintiff in the particular circumstances of the case in question. In short, the law expects people to take reasonable care in everything they do in order to avoid causing harm to others – to their 'neighbours'.

A defendant guilty of negligence does not necessarily intend to cause harm but may be found to be indifferent as to whether or not harm occurs. In *Blyth* v. *Birmingham Waterwork Co.* (1856) 11 Ex 781, negligence was defined as 'the omission to do something which a reasonable man would do or the doing of something which a reasonable man would not do'. This is perhaps an oversimplified view of the law of negligence. How can the plaintiff succeed in an action against the defendant? The plaintiff must prove the following four requirements:

● The defendant owed the plaintiff a duty to take care (known in law as the 'duty of care').
● The defendant's act or omission amounted to a breach of that duty.
● The defendant could have foreseen, or ought reasonably to have foreseen, that their act or omission would probably cause harm to the plaintiff.
● The defendant's act or omission caused the plaintiff to suffer loss, injury or damage.

However careless, defendants are not legally liable in the tort of negligence unless they owed the plaintiff a legal duty of care. The legal duty of care entails the use of such ordinary care and skill as is necessary in all the circumstances to avoid causing harm to anyone who is sufficiently 'close' to the defendant such that they ought to realize that the person would be injured if the defendant failed to take care. It is important to consider a number of questions when considering breach of the 'duty of care'. How much care should have been taken by the defendant and what constitutes reasonable care?

A leading case in negligence is that of *Donoghue* v. *Stevenson* [1932] AC 562 (previously referred to in Chapter 2). The plaintiff consumed a bottle of ginger beer purchased by a friend. The bottle contained what allegedly appeared to be the remains of a decomposed snail, the discovery of which caused the plaintiff's illness. The House of Lords held that the manufacturer of the ginger beer owed a duty of care to the ultimate consumer, irrespective of the lack of any contractual agreement between them. Since the plaintiff had suffered as a result of the manufacturer's alleged lack of care in ensuring that the product was fit for consumption, the manufacturer was guilty of negligence. In his judgement Lord Atkin stated that:

> any person who is so closely and directly affected by my act or omission that I ought reasonably to have them in my contemplation when directing my mind to the act or omission in question ... is my neighbour in the eyes of the law, and is owed a duty of care.

The standard of care which the law demands is that of the ordinary 'reasonable' person as is appropriate to the circumstances of each case.

Reasonable people are neither paragons nor clairvoyants. They possess average intelligence, skills and resources and have been described as the ordinary 'man on the Clapham omnibus' [1]. The test of reasonableness is an objective one, and the courts will usually take account of the common practices of society. The level of care required by the law may, however, change depending upon such issues as the particular facts of each case and whether or not the defendant professes to have, or the plaintiff could reasonably expect the defendant to have, special skills or abilities.

Two contrasting cases illustrate this point. In *Wells* v. *Cooper* [1958] 2 QB 265, the plaintiff was a visitor to the defendant's house. He fell and was injured when a door handle fixed by the defendant came away from the door in his hand. The court decided that the defendant was not negligent and therefore not liable for the plaintiff's injuries. The reasoning was that the standard of care owed was that of an ordinary man who was reasonably competent at carpentry and the court was satisfied on the evidence presented that this standard had been achieved.

The defendant in *Nettleship* v. *Weston* [1971] 2 QB 691 was a learner driver who collided with a lamp post, causing injury to the plaintiff, the driving instructor. The Court of Appeal came to the conclusion that the defendant owed the same standard of care to the plaintiff as a reasonably fully qualified and experienced driver. Since this standard had not been achieved the defendant was liable. It was no defence to say that the defendant was doing her incompetent best as an inexperienced driver.

However, the law does not require the highest possible degree of care. The standard of care depends upon the seriousness of the injury risked and the likelihood of the injury occurring. This point is well illustrated in the following cases.

The plaintiff in *Paris* v. *Stepney Borough Council* [1951] AC 367 worked in a garage owned by the defendants. While using a hammer to remove a bolt from a vehicle, the plaintiff was struck in the eye and blinded by a splinter of metal. Since he was already blind in the other eye the result was obviously devastating. It was alleged that the defendants were negligent in not providing goggles. In their defence the defendants brought evidence to show that it was customary practice at that time for employers not to provide eye protection. The House of Lords, however, held that the defendants were negligent and consequently liable for the plaintiff's injuries. They owed a higher standard of care to this particular defendant because of the increased seriousness of the potential injury risked.

Contrast this decision with the case of *Bolton* v. *Stone* [1951] AC850 where Miss Stone was hit and injured by a cricket ball hit out of the ground by a batsman during an ordinary game of cricket. It was alleged that the cricket club was negligent in not providing a fence sufficiently high to prevent such accidents. In the ensuing court case it was held that the cricket club was not negligent. Lord Oaksey stated that although a reasonable man would foresee the possibility of many risks, it would be impossible for him to take precautions against every conceivable risk that might occur, and the law expects him only to take precautions against risks which are reasonably likely to happen.

It is particularly significant to the built environment professions that a person claiming to be an expert in any particular trade or profession owes a duty of care to those reasonably likely to be affected by their acts or omissions while practising their calling. The law requires that such a person must consider all relevant factors and exercise the care and skill of an ordinary, competent practitioner usually engaged in that trade or profession. Inexperience is no defence.

For example, in *Kenny* v. *Hall Pain and Foster* (1976) 239 EG 355 the defendant's inexperience in valuing property of the type purchased by the plaintiffs, who had relied upon the valuer's advice, was no defence to a claim in negligence when it later transpired that the property had been overvalued causing the plaintiff financial loss. The decision in part stems from the statement by Lord Morris in *Hedley Byrne and Co. Ltd* v. *Heller and Partners* [1964] AC 465 in which he said that 'if someone possessing a special skill undertakes ... to apply that skill for the assistance of another who relies on such skill, a duty of care arises'. There can, however, be no liability if the damage suffered by the plaintiff is too remote from the act or omission of the defendant. The defendant will be liable only for such damage as in all the circumstances was reasonably foreseeable. If a reasonably minded person in the same position as the defendant could have predicted (without the need for 'supernatural powers') the outcome of the defendant's conduct, had they applied their mind to it, then the defendant will be liable for such injuries or damage as the plaintiff suffers which can be directly attributed to that conduct [2].

The defendant may also be liable for any particular damage suffered by the plaintiff beyond that which the average person might suffer, where the plaintiff is particularly sensitive or susceptible to the type of injury caused by the defendant's negligence.

In *Smith* v. *Leech Brain and Co. Ltd* [1962] 2 QB, the plaintiff was the widow of an employee of the defendants. Her husband died of a particular form of cancer to which he was susceptible and which had been aggravated by a burn caused by the negligence of his employers. Although the burn itself would not have necessarily killed an 'average' person, the court had no hesitation in finding the defendants liable for the death on the basis that the defendant 'must take his victim as he finds him'.

Plaintiffs who fail to establish the necessary breach of a duty of care owed by the defendant will fail in their action. There are, however, various defences available even if breach of a duty of care is established.

VOLENTI NON FIT INJURIA ('CONSENT')

A plaintiff who consents to run the risk of harm occasioned by the defendant's reasonable conduct cannot expect a remedy if indeed harm is suffered.

As Lord Herschell put it in *Smith* v. *Baker* [1891] AC 325 at 360, 'one who has invited or assented to an act being done towards him cannot, when he suffers from it, complain if it was a wrong'.

The test is an objective one as to whether the plaintiff gave consent freely, in the knowledge of the possible injury. The plaintiff, however, can never be said to consent to the defendant's negligent action. In *Slater* v. *Clay Cross Co. Ltd* [1956] 2 QB 264, the plaintiff was injured while lawfully walking through a tunnel on a railway track owned and occupied by the defendants. The injury was the result of negligent driving by the defendant's employee. The defence of *volenti* was raised, to which Lord Denning (dismissing the defence) said that 'when this lady walked in the tunnel ... she voluntarily took the risk of danger from the running of the railway in the ordinary way ... she did not take the risk of negligence by the driver'. Consent therefore can only be genuinely given to the risk of harm likely to be caused by the defendant who is acting reasonably and responsibly in all the circumstances. If the defendant is not acting reasonably or responsibly then it seems that the defence of consent is not available.

NOVUS ACTUS INTERVENIENS

If there is some interruption in the link between the defendant's alleged negligence and the plaintiff's injury it might be possible to claim successfully that the defendant is not responsible for the injury on the basis that the damaged suffered is too remote from the cause in action.

CONTRIBUTORY NEGLIGENCE

Section 1(1) Law Reform (Contributory Negligence) Act 1945 provides that:

> where any person suffers damage as a result partly of his own fault and partly of the fault of another person or persons, a claim in respect of that damage shall not be defeated by reason of the fault of the person suffering the damage but the damages recoverable in respect therefrom shall be reduced to such an extent as the court thinks just and equitable having regard to the plaintiff's share in the responsibility for the damage.

For example, in *Froom* v. *Butcher* [1976] QB 286, the plaintiff's damages were reduced because his injuries sustained as a passenger in the car negligently driven by the defendant were made worse by the fact that he was not wearing a seat belt.

Finally, to be successful at all a plaintiff must bring an action in the courts within the limitation period. Under the Limitation Act 1980 the action must be brought within six years of the defendant's act or omission which has caused the injury. In cases of personal injury the limitation period is three years from the date the injury is sustained.

The Latent Damage Act 1986 extended the limitation period in the case of latent defects which take time to materialize. The plaintiff has three years from the date that they had the knowledge required for bringing an action for damages, subject to a maximum period of 15 years from the date of the defendant's negligent act or omission [3].

STANDARD OF CARE

The standard of care in negligence is based on an objective test of reasonableness. It is not a static test and the standard changes depending upon the circumstances of each case. Consider three or four situations where the law demands a higher or lower standard of care from certain individuals.

TRESPASS

In the context of this work, reference to trespass is restricted to trespass on land. Trespass may be defined as the direct, deliberate and unauthorized interference with a person's possession of land.

An act of trespass is committed when the trespasser makes a conscious decision to enter on to another's land without permission or authority, or remains on land after any permission or authority granted has been revoked or lapsed [4].

It is also a trespass to place or leave objects on another's land without permission or authority. Trespass is actionable *per se*. It is not necessary for the plaintiff to prove that the defendant intended to commit damage or harm, nor that there was any reasonable foresight of possible damage or harm resulting from the trespass [5]. Consequently, it is not necessary to show that any damage has in fact been suffered. Similarly, defendants cannot justify their actions by claiming that they acted reasonably or with due care and were unaware of the fact that they had committed a trespass. In short, an act of trespass can be committed by a defendant who to all intents and purposes is 'innocent' of any charge of having any intention to do wrong. All that is necessary is to show that the defendant intended or freely volunteered to be on the plaintiff's land or to leave any object on the plaintiff's land without permission or authority. To a certain extent the defendant's motives are irrelevant.

It is the immediate and direct action of the defendant which constitutes the trespass. If the invasion of the plaintiff's land is merely a consequence of the defendant's acts or omissions there will be no trespass. In *Mann* v. *Saulnier* [6] a boundary fence for which the defendant was responsible collapsed and fell onto the plaintiff's land. Since the entry on to the plaintiff's land by the defendant's fence was a consequence of the collapse through lack of maintenance there was no trespass.

Placing a ladder against the plaintiff's wall is, however, a trespass [7], as is allowing a dog to run across someone else's land.

It is also a trespass to invade the airspace above the surface of the plaintiff's land without ever coming into contact with the ground or any buildings thereon. For example, in *Woollerton and Wilson Ltd* v. *Richard Costain*

[8] and also in *Anchor Brewhouse Developments Ltd* v. *Berkeley House (Docklands Developments) Ltd* [9] it was considered that an act of trespass would be committed by the jib of a tower crane swinging over the plaintiff's land. It is not a trespass to fly over the plaintiff's land at a 'reasonable' height having due regard to all the circumstances and weather conditions [10].

Unauthorized entry below the surface of the plaintiff's land at any depth will also constitute a trespass. Thus tunnelling through or digging into the subsoil below the plaintiff's land is actionable if such activity is carried out without the owner's consent.

The defendant in an action for trespass is obviously the person whose activity constitutes a direct invasion of and interference with another person's possession of land.

On the other hand the plaintiff is anyone with lawful right to immediate possession and control over the use of the land encroached upon. This includes freeholders, tenants, mortgagees whose right to possession of the land has arisen through default of the mortgagor and the owners of easements [12]. An owner of land who does not have an immediate right to possession or control over the land cannot sue. Thus a landlord cannot sue while there is a tenant in lawful occupation of the land. In such circumstances it is the tenant who has the right to possession and therefore the right to sue in trespass [13]. A landlord can, however, sue a tenant who remains in occupation of the land without lawful authority after the expiration of the lease. A tenant may indeed sue a landlord who enters the land under the tenant's control without lawful authority. Immediate possession usually means physical possession. Under the doctrine of 'trespass by relation', however, once a person with a right to take possession exercises that right and actually takes physical possession, they can sue in trespass anyone who has unlawfully entered the land in question between the date upon which the legal right to possession arose and physical possession was taken [14]. (Tenants do have many statutory rights which may give them some protection against such an action; for example, in the Rent Act 1977, Housing Act 1988 and Landlord and Tenant Act 1954.)

Misuse of a public highway for an unauthorized purpose may also constitute a trespass. The plaintiff in such cases is the owner of the subsoil below the surface of the highway. In most cases this is presumed to be the owner of the adjoining land, subject to the rights of the Highway Authority.

An occupier's right to physical possession and control and therefore the right to bring an action in trespass against unauthorized entry can only be defeated by the alleged trespasser proving themselves to be a dispossessed owner of the land who has better title to the land than the occupier, or that they are acting on behalf of someone with better title.

It is a criminal offence under s6 Criminal Law Act 1977 to use or threaten to use force in order to secure re-entry to property occupied by a trespasser. In such circumstances the dispossessed owner may either peacefully re-enter the property in order to evict the trespasser or bring an action for recovery.

An exception to this rule is that a dispossessed residential occupier may use reasonable force to enter and evict a trespasser from his/her property.

Finally, a plaintiff is prima facie entitled to an injunction to prevent or restrain a continuing trespass.

What if any defences are there to an action in trespass?

It may be a defence to claim that it was necessary to enter the plaintiff's land without permission in order to protect life or property or in the public interest to prevent some greater harm. In such circumstances the defendant must show that (s)he acted out of necessity, and that the alleged trespass was therefore in all the circumstances a reasonable course of action to take.

WORKPIECE 8.2

TORTS

Consider what tort(s) may have been committed and the defendant's possible liability and/or defence in the following situations.

● The defendant was the pilot of a hot-air balloon that landed without permission in the plaintiff's field. Weather conditions were good and the pilot was not making a forced landing. No damage was caused to the plaintiff's field.

● The defendant entered the plaintiff's field in order to rescue a hot-air balloon that had crash-landed and was drifting out of control. The pilot was injured in the landing. Damage was caused to the plaintiff's crops in an effort to prevent more extensive damage being caused by the balloon.

NUISANCE

Nuisance may be defined as an unreasonable interference with an individual's use of land or their enjoyment of some right over land. Although this chapter will deal predominantly with liability in private nuisance, it should be noted that nuisance can also be public and statutory. As an individual tort, nuisance exists as a control mechanism in order to balance the competing interests of neighbouring land users. It aims to balance the right of individuals to use their own land as they wish with that of their neighbours who do not wish to be unreasonably disturbed. Consequently, liability in nuisance revolves around what is considered to be reasonable in the circumstances. In order to establish whether or not a nuisance has occurred, the courts will apply a number of tests. These tests are not conclusive and not all will be relevant in each case. What are these tests?

LOCATION

It is suggested that the location in which an alleged nuisance takes place will always be significant. Certain uses of land are considered entirely reasonable in a given location. For example, one would expect to experience a certain level of noise, smell and smoke in an industrial area but not on a residential estate. In *Sturges* v. *Bridgman* (1879) 11 ChD 852 the court held that noise and vibration emanating from the defendant's use of his premises for making confectionery constituted a nuisance. In arriving at this decision, the court took into account the fact that predominant use in that location was for doctors' consulting rooms and made the point that 'what is a nuisance in Belgrave Square is not necessarily so in Bermondsey'.

The mere fact that a given location is renowned for a certain activity will not be an automatic defence where an interference is over and above what would be considered reasonable. In *Rushmer* v. *Polsue & Alfieri Ltd* (1906), the House of Lords upheld the plaintiff's claim for an injunction against the defendant's use of a printing press despite the fact that the premises were situated in the prime printing area in London. This was because the noise from the printing press was excessive despite the location.

CONTINUITY/DURATION

An underlying principle of nuisance is that the activity complained of is of a sufficient continuity. This will depend upon the facts and circumstances in each individual case. In *Bolton* v. *Stone* (1951) AC 850 the plaintiff was injured on the highway by a cricket ball which had been hit out of the defendant's ground. The evidence showed that such an event had occurred only six times in the past 30 years and was held to be too infrequent to constitute a nuisance.

SENSITIVITY OF THE PLAINTIFF

As the test for nuisance is an objective one, an over-sensitive plaintiff is unlikely to succeed as the alleged nuisance would not have interfered with the use or enjoyment of land by 'the reasonable man'. This principle is extended to include an over-sensitive use of property, so that in *Robinson* v. *Kilvert* (1889) 41 ChD 88 AC the defendant was not liable for the damage caused to the plaintiff's paper by heat produced by the defendant's manufacturing processes. The damage was due to the sensitivity of the particular type of paper rather than to the defendant's use.

Unlike negligence, the tort of nuisance is not concerned with fault, and the conduct of the defendant is often irrelevant. However, where the defendant has acted maliciously, this may be used as evidence of unreasonableness. In *Christie* v. *Davey* (1893) 1 Ch 316, the plaintiff gave music lessons in the house, upsetting the defendant. In order to show his displeasure, the defendant banged tin trays on the party wall and shouted whilst the lessons were being given. The court held that the defendant's malicious conduct constituted a nuisance and granted an injunction to the plaintiff, restraining the defendant's behaviour.

CONDUCT OF THE DEFENDANT

There has been a difference of judicial opinion as to whether public utility should be a factor to be considered by the court in deciding whether the defendant is liable in nuisance. In *Miller* v. *Jackson* (1977) QB 966, cricket balls were hit into the plaintiff's garden from the adjacent cricket club. The club had made extensive efforts to prevent this occurrence and Lord Denning expressed the view that, as the general public benefited from the activity, it should not constitute a nuisance. This view was not shared by the remainder of the Court of Appeal who found the defendant liable. However, the public factor was taken into account by the court in deciding not to grant an injunction.

PUBLIC UTILITY

As private nuisance is concerned with the unreasonable interference with a person's use or enjoyment of their land, it follows that only those with a legal interest in the land can sue. This normally comprises occupants who either own the freehold interest or have a tenancy. The leading authority on this point is *Malone* v. *Laskey* (1907) 2 KB 141 CA, where the wife of a tenant was injured by a defective cistern which had been dislodged by vibrations on the defendant's premises. It was held that she was unable to bring an action in nuisance as she had no proprietary or possessory interest in the land. It should be noted, however, that a person who is not in occupation can bring an action as long as it can be established that some permanent injury to the landlord's reversionary interest, for example, is being caused.

WHO CAN SUE?

In the majority of cases, the defendant to the action will be the creator of the alleged nuisance and also the occupier of the property on which the disturbance takes place. However, the following decisions should be noted as examples of situations where this is not necessarily the case.

WHO CAN BE SUED?

● In *Mint* v. *Good* (1951) 1 KB 517, the landlord of premises let on a weekly tenancy was held to be liable for injury caused by a defective wall as there was an implied obligation upon the landlord to maintain the premises.

● In *Sedleigh Demfield* v. *O'Callaghan* (1940) AC 880, the occupier was held to be liable for a nuisance created by a third party. Pipework had been installed in a ditch on the occupier's land by the county council without having given notice of any kind. When the ditch became blocked and caused a neighbour's land to become flooded, it was held that the occupier was liable in nuisance as no steps had been taken to prevent the blockage arising, despite the knowledge that the pipework had been installed.

● In *Tetley* v. *Chitty* (1986) 1 All ER 663, the defendant council had given consent to a go-kart club to use its land. An action was brought by local residents due to the excessive noise. The council's defence that it had not created the nuisance failed. It had allowed the club to use the land and had therefore expressly or by implication authorized the nuisance.

DEFENCES

It should be recognized that the most obvious way of defending an action in nuisance is to prove that the disturbance is not unreasonable in the circumstances with reference to the tests outlined earlier. However, certain specific principles need to be considered under this heading.

COMING TO THE NUISANCE   It is no defence to argue that the plaintiff moved to the nuisance. In *Sturges* v. *Bridgman* (1879), the defendant claimed that the doctor who built the consulting rooms was aware of the noise from the defendant's adjacent premises and had therefore come to the nuisance. This argument was rejected by the court. Similarly, in *Bliss* v. *Hall* (1838) 4 BING NC 183, the plaintiff complained of certain 'noxious and foul smells' coming from the defendant's premises, which were used for candle making. The defence was that this activity had been carried on prior to the plaintiff taking residence. It was held that this was no defence and judgement was given for the plaintiff.

'PRESCRIPTION'   It is a defence to show that the alleged nuisance has been carried on for a period of 20 years or more and that the plaintiff has been aware of this and had the opportunity of bringing an action. This argument was used by the defendant confectioner in *Sturges* v. *Bridgman* but was dismissed by the court as his activities became a nuisance only when the new consulting rooms were built. The defence failed for the same reason in *Miller* v. *Jackson* (1977) as the playing of cricket became a nuisance only once the residential estate had been built and subsequently occupied by the residents.

STATUTORY AUTHORITY   No liability in nuisance will arise where an activity is authorized by statute as long as the disturbance is reasonable in view of the provisions of the statute and in the absence of negligence; *Allen* v. *Gulf Oil Refining Co.* (1981) AC 1001.

In the vast majority of nuisance actions, the remedy granted is an injunction which forces the defendant to terminate the activities. This is an equitable remedy and the court has the discretion not to award an injunction in those circumstances outlined in *Shelfer* v. *City of London Electric Lighting Co.* (1895) 1 Ch 287 CA:

REMEDIES

- Where the injury to the plaintiff's legal right:
  - is small;
  - is capable of being estimated in money terms;
  - is one which can be adequately compensated by a small money payment.
- Where it would be oppressive to the defendant to grant an injunction.

WORKPIECE 8.3

NUISANCE

Richard is a law lecturer who often works from home because of the peace and quiet. He recently moved to a cottage on the edge of a small market town a few miles from the university where he teaches. Half a mile away from his cottage is a factory which employs most of the local residents. The factory has occupied its current site for 50 years. Employees work eight-hour shifts throughout the day and night and a hooter is sounded to summon them to work. The hooter sounds for 60 seconds at 6.45 a.m., 2.45 p.m. and 10.45 p.m. every day except Sundays. On occasion when the wind is from a certain direction Richard can hear the general noise from the factory and there is the occasional smell. Richard finds all this very distracting, particularly as he is a very light sleeper and has had several sleepless nights recently. He has asked the factory owners to modify their working practices but they have refused. Consider the position of Richard and identify what legal remedies, if any, he might have.

WORKPIECE 8.4

NUISANCE AND LANDLORDS

Consider in what circumstances a landlord might be held liable for a nuisance committed by his tenant.

THE RULE IN *RYLANDS* V. *FLETCHER*

The rule was developed by the judiciary to impose liability upon those landowners for damage caused as a result of an escape from their land. The effect is one of strict liability which means that, once damage has been established, the defendant is liable irrespective of fault.

In *Rylands* v. *Fletcher* (1868) LR 1 Ex Ch 265, the defendant employed independent contractors to construct a reservoir on his land. The contractors failed to discover disused mine shafts located on the land and, when the reservoir was filled, water escaped and flooded the plaintiff's adjoining colliery. The court held that the defendant was liable and laid down the following rule:

> Where a person for his own purpose brings and keeps on land in his occupation anything likely to do mischief if it escapes, he must keep it in at his peril, and if he fails to do so he is prima facie answerable for all damage which is the natural consequence of its escape.

ESTABLISHING LIABILITY

ACCUMULATION The rule in *Rylands* v. *Fletcher* applies only to things which are artificially brought onto the land and not to those which naturally accumulate there. For this reason, in *Leakey* v. *National Trust for Places of Historic Interest or Natural Beauty* (1980) QB 485, the rule did not apply to land owned by the defendant which cracked due to weathering, causing a major collapse of earth on to and the consequential damage to the plaintiff's land.

ESCAPE It must be shown that injury arose as a result of an escape from premises. In *Read* v. *J. Lyons & Co. Ltd* (1947) AC 156, the plaintiff was employed in the defendant's munitions factory and was injured as a result of an explosion. It was held that the rule did not apply as the plaintiff had been inside the premises at the time of the explosion and there had not been an escape from the defendant's land. The court stated that, for the purposes of the rule, escape meant 'escape from a place where the defendant has occupation of or control over land to a place which is outside his occupation or control'.

NON-NATURAL USE OF LAND It is evident from authorities which have followed Rylands that the rule applies only to non-natural uses of land. This principle stems from the words of Blackburn J who referred to those things 'naturally on the land and not artificially created' and, although there was initial uncertainty amongst the judiciary, it is now apparent that this encompasses uses which would not ordinarily occur given all the circumstances of the case.

In *Mason* v. *Levy Auto Parts of England Ltd* (1967) 2 QB 530, the defendant stored a considerable amount of combustible materials on his premises. When a fire broke out and spread to the plaintiff's premises, an action was brought under the *Rylands* v. *Fletcher* principle. In deciding that the defendant's use was non-natural, the court took into account the way in which the materials were stored, the quantities stored and the nature of the locality.

Conversely, in *Rickards* v. *Lothian* (1913) AC 263, the defendant was held to be not liable under Rylands for damage caused to the plaintiff's property by water which escaped from a tap which had been turned on by a stranger on the defendant's premises. The use to which the defendant put the premises was held to be ordinary and, as Lord Moulton stated, 'it must be some special use bringing with it increased danger to others' as opposed to the ordinary everyday use of land.

DAMAGE The rule in *Rylands* v. *Fletcher* is not a tort actionable *per se*. In other words, the plaintiff must prove that some damage has resulted from the escape if the defendant is to be liable. The extent of the defendant's liability is unclear. The test is either one of directness, i.e. everything which is a direct consequence of the escape can be claimed, or one of foreseeability, i.e. only that kind of damage which could reasonably have been foreseen is recoverable. This is a complex argument and it is submitted, for now, that the former test is more applicable to a tort of strict liability.

DEFENCES

Although liability in Rylands is said to be strict, it is not absolute in that there are a number of available defences.

DEFAULT OF THE PLAINTIFF If it can be shown that the plaintiff was entirely responsible for the damage, he will have no action. If, however, the plaintiff is contributorily negligent, his damages will be reduced by an amount which takes into account that contribution.

CONSENT OF THE PLAINTIFF If the plaintiff has expressly or by implication consented to the presence of the thing on the defendant's land or it has been brought onto the land partly for the plaintiff's benefit, the defendant is not liable for damage resulting from an escape unless the defendant has been negligent. For example, in *Peters* v. *Prince of Wales Theatre*

(Birmingham) Ltd [1943] KB 73, the plaintiff occupied shop premises leased from the defendant. The defendant had installed a sprinkler system in the whole property including the plaintiff's shop. When freezing weather caused water to pour out of the system and into the plaintiff's premises, damaging his stock, he sued both in negligence and under *Rylands* v. *Fletcher.* The court held that the defendant had not been negligent and was not liable under Rylands as the sprinkler system had been installed for their common benefit and with the knowledge of the plaintiff.

ACT OF GOD   Where the damage is due to extreme natural circumstances which could not reasonably have been foreseen, the defendant will not be liable. In *Nichols* v. *Marsland* (1876) 2 EXDI, CA, such circumstances comprised severe rainstorms 'greater and more violent than any within with memory of witnesses' but it should be noted that this defence has a limited application today.

ACT OF A THIRD PARTY   Where the escape and resultant damage is caused by the unforeseeable act of a third party, the defendant will not be liable. The third party must be a stranger if the defence is to succeed, as its essence is derived from the defendant's total lack of control in the circumstances (see *Richards* v. *Lothian*, above).

STATUTORY AUTHORITY   Defendants will not be liable where they are acting in pursuance of powers conferred by statute as long as they have not been negligent. In *Green* v. *Chelsea Waterworks Co.* (1894) 70 LT 547, the plaintiff's premises were flooded when the defendant's water main burst. The court held that the defendant possessed statutory authority to provide a water supply and that as bursts were inevitable from time to time, the defendant was not liable.

WORKPIECE 8.5

STRICT LIABILITY

The rule in *Rylands* v. *Fletcher* is one of strict liability. Discuss what this means and consider the effectiveness of the defences.

WORKPIECE 8.6

RYLANDS V. *FLETCHER* AND ITS LINKS TO VARIOUS TORTS

What common theme, if any, links the torts of negligence, trespass nuisance and *Rylands* v. *Fletcher*?

As society becomes increasingly more complex so it is necessary to ensure that the law operates in a manner that seeks to achieve a balance between any conflicting interests. The law not only confers certain rights on individuals but also may impose certain obligations.

    The legal relationship between individuals that may subsequently arise is the basis of the law of tort.

    This chapter has:

SUMMARY

- examined the torts of negligence, trespass and nuisance;
- explored the potential areas of conflict and how the law is used to resolve them;
- looked in particular at the rule in *Rylands* v. *Fletcher*.

After reading this chapter, you will:

CHECKLIST

- understand how tortious liability arises at law;
- understand the legal principles which apply to the torts of negligence, trespass, nuisance and *Rylands v.* Fletcher;
- appreciate the defences applicable to these torts.

REFERENCES

1. *Hall* v. *Brooklands Auto Racing Club* [1933] 1KB 205, 217).
2. *Overseas Tankship (UK) Ltd* v. *Marts Dock and Engineering Co. Ltd (The* Wagon *Mound)* [1961] AC 388 and *Overseas Tankship (UK) Ltd* v. *Miller Steamship Co Pty Ltd (The Wagon Mound No 2)* [1967] 1 AC 617.
3. *Spencer-Ward and another* v. *Humberts* [1995] 06 EG 148.
4. *Minister of Health* v. *Bellotti* (1944) KB 298.
5. *Entick* v. *Carrington* (1765) 2 Wils KB 275.
6. (1959) 19 DLR (2d) 130.
7. *Westripp* v. *Baldock* (1938) 2 All ER 779.
8. (1970) 1 WLR 411.
9. (1987) 38 BLR 82.
10. *Bernstein of Leigh (Baron)* v. *Skyviews and General Ltd* (1978) QB 479 and 576 Civil Aviation Act 1982.
11. *Bulli Coal Mining Co.* v. *Osborne* (1899) AC 351.
12. *Hill* v. *Tupper* (1863) 2 H and C 121.
13. *Jones* v. *Llanrwst U.D.C.* (1911) 1 Ch 393.
14. *Barnett* v. *Earl of Guildford* (1855) 11 Exch 19.

FURTHER READING

Brazer, M. (1993) *Street on Torts*, 9th edn, Butterworths.
Cole, J. (1995) *Law of Tort*, 2nd edn, Pitman Publishing.
Fleming, J. (1988) *The American Tort Process*, Clarendon, Oxford.

Horn, N., Kotz, H. and Leser, H. (1982) *German Private and Commercial Law*, Clarendon, Oxford.

Murdoch, C. and Schofield, P. (1994) *Law for Estate Management Students*, 4th edn, Butterworths.

LAND AND LAND LAW

JAN RUSSELL

THEME

The built environment consists of man-made structures on land. It is essential for anyone living or working within this environment to understand the legal mechanisms that operate which allow acquisition and ownership of land and the rights of third parties. Different countries have different legal mechanisms and hence the implications for personal or business activities will vary. This chapter seeks to examine the situation in England and Wales, focusing on a range of issues including estates and interests, co-ownership, mortgages, restrictive covenants, easements and adverse possession. It also encompasses land registration and third-party rights. The subject is so complex that it is intended merely to provide a brief introduction to the main areas that a student of the built environment is likely to meet.

OBJECTIVES

After reading this chapter you should be able to:

● understand the two estates in land;

● appreciate the difference between an estate and an interest;

● distinguish between easements, restrictive covenants and licences;

● understand how mortgages work;

● appreciate the effects of third-party rights on land;

● identify where situations concerning adverse possession may arise.

INTRODUCTION

Land is complicated because many people can have different interests in one piece of land. The following example attempts to demonstrate this wide range of interests.

Bill owns a leasehold house which he is buying with the aid of a mortgage. He lives in the house with his wife Bella. They have rented out a spare room to a student from a nearby university. Bill wants to set up a dental practice from his home but has been told that there is a term in his deeds which prevents him doing so. Bella wants to extend the property by having a conservatory built; however, the neighbours complain that it would block the light to their kitchen. Their drive is a shared drive with the next-door-neighbour, Fred. Fred keeps blocking the drive with his old cars.

This scenario gives an idea of the range of issues dealt with in land law.

Partly because of the value of the property, it is important that the legal issues are clarified. An additional complication sometimes occurs because land owned by an individual may get caught up in an informal family arrangement made without regard to the law. This is fine in theory but, when the relationship founders, the informal arrangement must be resolved by a rigid legal system that finds it difficult to cope equitably and consistently with family arrangements.

For example, *Greasley* v. *Cooke* [1980] [1]: Ms Cooke was employed as resident maid in a large family home. She later formed a relationship with a son of the family and continued to live in the house, acting as unpaid housekeeper. She was assured, when the original employer died and the house was inherited by her lover and his siblings, that she could continue to live in the house for as long as she wanted. The family later changed their minds. The court held that her reliance on the assurances raised an equity in her favour allowing her to remain in the property despite the fact that she had no recognized legal footing as owner or tenant.

ESTATES IN LAND

Since 1066, all land has been technically owned by the crown but there are two ways of holding, as opposed to owning, land in England and Wales. What are these two estates in land?

A **freehold** is technically known as a **fee simple absolute in possession** and is an estate which lasts indefinitely.

The other estate is a **lease**, otherwise known as a **term of years**, which lasts for that period determined in the lease. An interest in land is the enforceable right someone else has over your land such as, for example, an easement to drain his surface water into your drains, a right of way to cross your property or a restrictive covenant preventing a house being converted for business use.

One of the most important issues in relation to interests in land is whether or not these interests will continue after the land has changed hands. The usual rule is that as long as the prospective purchaser has notice of the right when he buys, he will buy subject to that right. A good case to illustrate this point is that of *Tulk* v. *Moxhay* [1848] [2]. Tulk sold land in Leicester Square to Mr Elms on the proviso that he did not build there. Elms sold it on to Moxhay, who knew of the building restriction and bought it cheaply as a result. Moxhay decided to ignore the restriction on the basis that he was not a party to the agreement. The court held that he was nevertheless bound by it because it would be inequitable for him to have the benefit of a low price due to the building restriction, and then be able to ignore it. Moxhay was bound by the doctrine of notice, which has these days been generally replaced by entries in the various statutory registers.

It is important therefore to consider what is meant by **registration of land**. When land is bought, freehold or leasehold, the property is transferred under the Land Registration Act 1925. Most land in this country is now registered with the Land Registry, which issues a land certificate for each plot. The certificate includes a description of the land, the owners and a list of charges that are registered as affecting the land. The idea behind the system was that the land certificate would mirror what was happening on the land and that the document would simply be the only legal information required, existing much as a log book does for a car. However, s70 of the Land Registration Act 1925 lists the overriding interests which will bind a purchaser, despite the fact that the purchaser may have no knowledge of their existence because they do not appear on the register. The most common and difficult to deal with is covered under the section on co-ownership whereby more than one person will purchase land.

When more than one person purchases land, the law has determined how the land should be held. There are two types of co–ownership: joint tenancy and tenancy in common, but only **joint tenancy** is recognized in law by the Law of Property Act 1925.

The key features of joint tenancy are the four unities of time, title, interest and possession; another feature is the right of survivorship. The four unities can be explained as follows. The **unity of possession** means that each of the tenants is entitled to possession of the whole of the

CO-OWNERSHIP

147

land, i.e. it is not divided into parts. The **unity of interest** means that the nature, duration and extent of the holding should be the same. The **unity of title** requires that the title of each joint tenant must be created by the same document of title, i.e. the same conveyance, and the **unity of time** means that the interest should vest at the same time. The effect of the **right of survivorship** (or *jus accrescendi*) is that on the death of one joint tenant, the other surviving joint tenants will inherit his share of the property automatically. This arrangement overrides any will left by a joint tenant which purports to leave his share of the property to any other party. This is obviously acceptable in a standard matrimonial home when, for example, on the death of the husband he would want his widow to inherit. However, it is not a satisfactory arrangement for business partners who would prefer that their property pass to their next of kin rather than to their business partner. For this reason, equity recognizes **tenancy in common**, allowing a tenant in common's share of the property to be inherited by the next of kin or person otherwise nominated in the will. Tenants in common cannot exist on the title deeds of the property so all property that is co-owned must be co-owned as a joint tenancy. The legal estate is also said to be held on trust for sale imposed by S34 & 35 L.P.Act 1925. It is the equitable or beneficial interest that can be held as a tenancy in common.

This arrangement protects purchasers who need be concerned only with the legal estate. As long as the purchasers obtain the signatures of the trustees on the transfer documents, then the interest of any beneficial owners are overreached or transferred to proceeds of sale. This arrangement will overcome a problem caused by s70(1)(g) of the Land Registration Act 1925, where the co-ownership arose and one partner is on the title deeds but the other is entitled to a share in the property in equity because they have made a substantial contribution to the property. One of the commonest overriding interests is the right of a person in actual occupation under s70(1)(g).

In the case of *Williams and Glyns Bank v. Boland* [1981] [3], it was decided by the House of Lords that the wife had acquired an equitable interest in her husband's property by making a substantial contribution. This, along with her actual occupation of the matrimonial home, gave her an overriding interest having priority over a legal charge created by the husband after the wife had qualified for an overriding interest. This meant that the husband's mortgagees' claim to possession of the house was defeated by the wife's overriding interest. The rights of overriding interests can be overreached by purchasing from two or more vendors who are acting as trustees. The doctrine of overreaching will operate to transfer the interest from the land into the proceeds of sale.

In *City of London Building Society* v. *Flegg* [1988] [4], two couples (a daughter, her husband and her parents) bought a house together. The property was put in the names of the daughter and son-in-law but all four contributed to the purchase price and all four lived in the property. Therefore the daughter and son-in-law held the property on trust for sale for themselves and the older couple. A **trust for sale** is an automatic statutory trust that arises on co-ownership. When the daughter and son-in-law were declared bankrupt, the mortgagees, the City of London Building Society, took possession and priority over the parents because, under s2(i) of the Law of Property Act 1925, the rights of the parents were overreached by the payment of the mortgage money to the two trustees, i.e. the daughter and son-in-law. Therefore the parents lost their rights in the property, those rights being transferred instead to the money held by the daughter and son-in-law.

The arrangement of co-ownership can change during the existence of the ownership. If, for example, a husband and wife buy a house when they are happily married, they will often buy it as joint tenants in law and equity. However, if the relationship breaks down, then either party may sever the joint tenancy in equity, creating a tenancy in common. This severance can be done most effectively by unilateral notice in writing. If a dispute arises whereby one of the co-owners wishes to sell and the other does not, then any person interested can apply to the court under section 30 of the Law of Property Act 1925 and the court can exercise its discretion as to whether to order the sale. The presumption will be that if there is a dispute, then the property should be sold, but this presumption will be rebutted if it can be shown that the purpose of the trust is still being fulfilled.

In *Re Buchanan-Wollastons Conveyance* [1939] [5], four neighbours bought a piece of land to preserve it as open space. Later, one neighbour wanted the land sold but the court looked at the purpose of the purchase, established that it was still valid and refused the request for sale.

WORKPIECE 9.1

CO-OWNERSHIP

Wendy, Peter, John and Michael buy a property to live in while at college. How will they hold the property and what would happen if Peter fails at the end of the first year and wants to sell up but the others wish to remain?

MORTGAGES

It is common practice to borrow money in order to buy a property. The property is then used as security for the loan, e.g. it is mortgaged to the lender, be they bank or building society. The law relating to mortgages is complicated because of its historical basis. In the days when most of the population was in private rented accommodation, mortgages were used rarely and were generally only short-term loans.

The usual way to create a mortgage these days is by deed under s87 of the Law of Property Act 1925. The ownership of the mortgaged property remains with the mortgagor (borrower); the lender (mortgagee) acquires an interest in the property. This interest will be noted on the title document in the Land Registry called a 'charge certificate'.

What are the implications of creating a mortgage? The mortgagor's most important right is the right to redeem the property free of the mortgage; in other words, to pay off the mortgage. This is generally not a problem with residential mortgages but where a commercial mortgage is granted there may be other motives behind the loan which will mean that the mortgagee does not want to be repaid too early. For example, if a brewery loans money for the purchase of a pub, it will be on the express agreement that the pub will sell the brewery's product. It is not in the brewer's interest that the loan should be repaid early if it means that the 'solus' agreement (tying the pub to purchase only the brewer's products) will come to an end. These agreements conflict with the requirement that there shall be no 'clogs on the equity of redemption' but they can be mutually beneficial. The courts allow them as long as they are not too onerous and as long as there was not undue inequality of bargaining power. In *Fairclough* v. *Swan Brewery Co. Ltd* [1912] [6], the mortgaged property was a lease of 17½ years. The terms of the mortgage meant that the mortgagor could not redeem the mortgage until six weeks before the lease was due to expire. The court held that this rendered the right to redeem illusory and of little use and therefore the court granted the mortgagor the right to redeem at an earlier date.

The main rights of the legal mortgagee include the right to sell (s101 Law of Property Act 1925). This will arise on the mortgagor's default of either a breach of covenant (for example, not to sublet without permission) or default in mortgage payments (such as interest being in arrears for two months).

The right of sale does not arise in any case until the first six months of the mortgage have elapsed. If the mortgagor has a good record in making repayments and has fallen into arrears only because of a temporary problem (for example, a period out of work) the mortgagor can ask the court to exercise its discretion under the Administration of Justice Acts of 1970 and 1973. They can delay giving the mortgagee possession of the property until the mortgagor has had an opportunity to pay off the arrears. A mortgagee who does exercise the power of sale may be liable in negligence if he fails to get the market value for the property. In the case of *Cuckmere Brick Co.* v. *Mutual Finance Ltd* [1971] [7], the mortgagee sold the mortgaged land without advertising that it had the benefit of planning permission for a hundred flats. The mortgagee was liable to pay compensation to the mortgagor.

Negative equity has been a feature of the housing market in recent years. This occurs when a property is worth less than the mortgage. This may have arisen because the property was bought at the height of the price boom with a 100% mortgage. If the property is repossessed by the mortgagee and the sale price is insufficient to pay the debt, then the mortgagor will still be liable for the amount outstanding. There is a covenant in the mortgage that the whole debt will be paid. Any deficit may be met by an insurance policy that the lending institution insisted that the mortgagor should take out. However, the insurance policy is generally for the benefit of the mortgagee, not the mortgagor. The insurance company could sue the mortgagor for the amount that they have had to pay to the mortgagee.

The mortgagee can appoint a receiver in the same circumstances as the power of sale becomes exerciseable. The receiver can recover income from the property and apply it to paying the outgoings on the building and the mortgage debts. This power can be used for commercial property and will particularly be used where the market for such property is depressed.

The rather Dickensian right to foreclose means that the ownership in the mortgaged property vests in the mortgagee without the mortgagor receiving any benefit of the equity in the property. Therefore, for a property worth £100 000 that is mortgaged for £50 000, if the mortgagee forecloses on the mortgagor's default the whole property becomes his without any need or obligation to compensate the mortgagor for the £50 000 the latter owned in the property. Because of this inherent unfairness, the courts will generally grant relief against foreclosure and order the property to be sold instead. When a mortgagee takes possession to sell the property on the default of the mortgagor, there are strict rules laid down regarding the proceeds of sale. Any prior mortgages should be paid off, the expenses relating to the sale must be paid, the capital and interest of the mortgagee who took the action will be paid and any surplus will go to the subsequent mortgagees or, if none, to the mortgagor (s105 Law of Property Act 1925).

An important issue for mortgagees is the order of priority of repayment in the event of the mortgagor having a number of mortgages and not having sufficient assets to cover all the debts. The rule is that the priority is determined, not by the date that the mortgages were created, but by the date they were registered on the Charges Register with the Land Registry.

WORKPIECE 9.2

MORTGAGES

Fred borrowed money from Easiloan Ltd to help him start his window-cleaning business. The loan was secured against his property Chez Nous. He fell off a ladder and hurt his back and was neither able to work for a time nor capable of paying the instalments to either Easiloan or to Albion Building Society who had lent him the money to buy his house.

Consider what options and responsibilities Easiloan have in relation to Fred, Chez Nous and Albion Building Society.

RESTRICTIVE COVENANTS

Use of land can be limited where the land is subject to a restrictive covenant. Restrictive covenants occur under two main circumstances:

- where a landowner has sold part of the land and retained the rest;
- where a developer has built an estate of houses and wants to impose the same restrictive covenants on all the houses for the benefit of everyone living on the estate.

Restrictive covenants must be differentiated from 'positive' covenants, which are rarely enforceable beyond the existing contractual parties.

A restrictive covenant is one that does not require money to be spent to maintain observance of it. It is important to look beyond the wording of the covenant to its actual effect. For example, a covenant not to leave a garden as an open plan area appears to be negative at first sight, but the effect of it is to force someone to pay money to build a fence or grow a hedge. Hence it is a positive covenant rather than restrictive.

There is no problem enforcing a restrictive covenant between the two original parties because of the contractual arrangements between them. The problems arise when the land has been passed on to successive owners and there is no contractual relationship between them. Restrictive covenants come within the exceptions of the rules of privity of contract. Successors in title can often benefit from, and be subject to, the restrictive covenants despite the lack of a contract.

To be able to enforce the restrictive covenant a person must prove that:

● they own the land to be benefited (*London County Council* v. *Allen* [1914]) [8];
● the covenant is restrictive, i.e. it does not require money spent to uphold it;
● it must have been originally intended to continue to exist even though the original parties have sold on (this is presumed by Law of Property Act 1925 s78, subject to contrary intention);
● the covenant touches and concerns the land, i.e. affects the value of the land.

The benefit of the covenant must have been passed to the new owner through the equitable rules of either annexation, assignment or as part of a building scheme as per *Elliston* v. *Reacher* [1908] [9]. **Annexation** occurs where the covenant is attached to the land and the land is sold (this is presumed to be the case by s78 Law of Property Act 1925). **Assignment** passes the benefit of the covenant to the individual purchasers. A **building scheme** allows owners of housing estates to have the benefit and burden of the restrictive covenants in their scheme even though the developer does not retain land.

To enforce a covenant, the covenantee must prove that in addition to having the benefit, the burden has passed to the current owner of the servient tenement. The burden will not run in common law but there are devices to side-step this problem. The most common way around it is to create a chain of indemnity. Where the original purchaser signed to the effect that they would be liable for any breach of covenant, it is common for their solicitor, when they sell, to require the new purchaser to indemnify the original covenantee in the event that the original covenantee be sued for breach of covenant. This has the effect of passing on the liability down the chain. Equity, via the Doctrine of *Tulk* v. *Moxhay* (1848) [2] (see earlier), allows the burden to be passed down because it is thought unfair to let a purchaser buy land knowing of a restrictive covenant, and therefore paying a reduced price, and then be able to disregard the restriction.

The rules laid down in *Tulk* v. *Moxhay* require that the covenant will not run unless it is proved that the covenant is negative, is of benefit to the dominant tenement, was intended to run with the land of the covenantor (now presumed by s79 Law of Property Act 1925) and that there is land capable of being benefited. In *Re Ballard's Conveyance* [1937]

[10], an estate of 1700 acres was not thought capable of being benefited by a covenant – it was too big. The covenant should have been worded to limit the effect of the covenant to the area that was capable of being affected by the restrictive covenant.

Planning permission and restrictive covenants are unconnected. Planning officers will not take account of any possible restrictive covenants when making their decisions. In the event of an enforceable restrictive covenant being breached, then enforcement is by way of an injunction in the County Court.

One of the problems with restrictive covenants is that, once imposed, they will stay there until positive action is taken to remove them. This means many outdated covenants are still mentioned in the Charges Registry of the Land Registry. The Lands Tribunal has the power to remove or modify them under s84 of the Law of Property Act 1925 if they are obsolete. However, action will not be taken by the Lands Tribunal against redundant covenants unless an application is brought before them. This is comparatively rare due to the costs involved, including the possibility that it may result in compensation being paid to the beneficiary of the covenant.

WORKPIECE 9.3

RESTRICTIVE COVENANTS

Grandad died owning a large single house in two hectares of land on the edge of a thriving market town. The planners will not give permission for housing in the next five years. Grandad's family want to sell the house now to realize some capital but they would like to be able to gain some benefit from any development on the land in the future. How could they go about ensuring that no development will take place without their being able to take some benefit from the rise in value of the land?

EASEMENTS

This is the right to use another person's land for a particular purpose, or to stop them doing something on the land; for example, a right of way or a right of support.

Four conditions are laid down in *Re Ellenborough Park* [1956] [11] before a right can become an easement:

- There must be a dominant easement which benefits from and can enforce the easement and a servient tenement which is subject to the easement.
- There must be benefit for the dominant tenement.
- The dominant and servient tenement must be owned or occupied by different people. If one owner of property uses part of their own

property to walk across (for example, the owner of a house walks across a paddock that they own), this will not create an easement but a quasi easement. The doctrine in *Wheeldon* v. *Burrows* (1879) [12] will operate to allow a quasi easement to mature into an easement on the disposal of the ownership of the house if the quasi easement's use was continuous and apparent and it is necessary to the reasonable enjoyment of the land.

● The right must be capable of being granted, i.e. there must be someone able to make the grant and it must be within the class of rights capable of being an easement. It must not be too vague. It must not generally give the right to possession of the land (see, for example, *Copeland* v. *Greenhalf* [1952] [13] in which the defendant's right to park vehicles on the plaintiff's land was held to be more in the nature of a claim for adverse possession than an easement).

Even if a right could be an easement, it cannot be enforced unless it has been acquired by the owner of the land to be benefited, i.e. the dominant land.

Acquisition can be by a number of methods, for example by grant or reservation. If a person is selling part of their land, they can reserve their right to walk across the part sold. Alternatively, they could grant an easement to the purchaser of the part sold to walk across the part they have retained.

One of the most common methods of acquisition is under the Prescription Act 1832 which allows a prescriptive right to be earned if the right has been used for between 20 and 40 years. If the 20-year period is relied on, the claim can be defeated by proof that the servient owner gave written permission. If the 40-year period of use is applied then the claim cannot be challenged.

Under s62 of the Law of Property Act 1925 all easements and other rights that appertain to the land automatically pass under the conveyance unless a contrary intention is expressed. This section means that there is no need to define all the rights transferring with the property.

If a conveyance (including a lease) fails to grant a right that is essential to the use of the property, then the courts can imply an easement of necessity to cover the omission. In *Wong* v. *Beaumont Property Trust Ltd* [1965] [14], the tenant of restaurant premises was required by health regulations to ventilate the food rooms. This required ducting to be fixed to the landlord's premises, which had not been allowed for in the lease. The court held that the tenants had a right to the ducting – an easement of necessity.

Easements can be extinguished by abandonment of the right, express release or where the dominant and servient tenements come into the same ownership.

Where there is a need to enter neighbouring property to do repairs (for example, to a gable end which abuts the boundary) and no easement exists, then an application can be made to the court under the Access to Neighbouring Land Act 1992. The court has the powers, in limited circumstances, to order a property owner to allow their neighbour onto their land to effect repairs. The court order will lay down the terms under which the entry on to the land can be made.

WORKPIECE 9.4

EASEMENTS

Robin and John have been neighbours for the past two decades. Because Robin does not drive, he has allowed John to park his collection of motorbikes on his drive. Robin has now sold his property to Marion who wants to park her C5 on the drive. She finds that there is no room because John is taking up the space.

Advise Marion.

ADVERSE POSSESSION

Adverse possession, or 'squatters rights', is based on the concept that for practical reasons there must be a time limit within which people can claim their ownership of property. If this was not the case, and as long as lineage could be proved, the Anglo-Saxons might well be able to reclaim their inheritance from the Norman invaders. Thus, in this country, if a person has been adversely possessing land for more than 12 years the courts, as a rule, will accept that he is the new owner and that the 'paper' owner only holds it on trust for him (Limitation Act 1980). The possession must be *nec vi, nec clam* and *nec precario* – without strength, stealth or permission. If permission is given, e.g. in the form of a licence, then that will defeat a claim for adverse possession. There must be a factor of 'ouster' in the actions of the adverse possessor. Thus in the case of *Boosey* v. *Davis* (1988) [15], the action of clearing the land, mending fences and grazing goats was not held to be sufficient ouster of the true owner.

To prove that the possession is adverse, it is necessary to show that the occupation for the preceding 12 years was contrary to the rights of the true or paper owner, i.e. the squatter had *animus possidendi* for the 12 years. In *Morrice* v. *Evans* (1989) [16], the Evanses had bought a house but part of the garden had not been conveyed to them. It was landlocked so they began to use it and occupied the greenhouse. However, when the son-in-law of the true owner told them to stop using the greenhouse, they complied with his wishes, thereby demonstrating that they were not acting with *animus possidendi* as true owners of the property. They therefore lost their claim for the land.

ADVERSE POSSESSION

Joe has recently bought a house and on inspecting the plans he has discovered that, during the gales of approximately 10 years ago, the fence between himself and the neighbour blew down and the neighbour re-erected it a metre into what should have been Joe's garden. He wants to know if he can make the neighbour reinstate the fence in its original position.

Advise Joe.

EUROPEAN LAND LAW

The continental system of land law differs in many ways from the English system. The French legal system is codified, unlike our use of statute and common law. One other difference between the French and English method of land holding is the subject of co-ownership. In England, if a couple buy a house a joint tenancy is agreed; when the first joint tenant dies, the survivor inherits the whole property. In France, when a couple buy a house it is traditional that when the first partner dies the property is divided between the survivor and any children of the relationship. This means that the children can force the sale of the property against the wishes of the surviving parent. To avoid this problem the co-owners can enter into a deed known as 'donation'. This deed allows the survivor a right that is not ownership, but is called *l'usufruit*, which allows the survivor the right to occupy or take the rents and profits for a determined period.

In Germany and Denmark property rights are protected by the constitution.

SUMMARY

Land, particularly land for development, is in short supply in this country and is a very expensive resource. As such, it is the subject of much litigation.

Many people may have rights in or over a piece of land. Most of those rights are discoverable by examining the title deeds, or information retained by the local authority. However, sometimes rights can be discovered only by a thorough inspection of the property. Overriding interests and easements can fall into this category. Particular difficulty can exist in domestic situations where land is occupied by adults who do not appear on the title deeds. They may well have an interest that will bind an unwary purchaser.

This chapter has:

- looked at the differences between estates and interests in land;
- distinguished between easements, restrictive covenants and license;
- examined how mortgages work;
- considered the effects of third party rights on land;
- explored situations where adverse possession may arise.

CHECKLIST

Land ownership is very complicated because of the variety of estates and interests in land that can be held concurrently.

- Ownership of freehold land lasts indefinitely. Leaseholds exist for a fixed period of time.
- Co-ownership is when more than one person owns land. It can take the form of a joint tenancy or a tenancy in common.
- Mortgages are loans secured on land.
- Landowners can be restricted, by their neighbours, in the way they use their land. The restrictions can take the form of restrictive covenants and easements.
- Adverse possession occurs when ownership rights are acquired by an occupier of land.

REFERENCES

1. *Greasley* v. *Cooke* [1980] 3 All ER 710.
2. *Tulk* v. *Moxhay* (1848) 2 Ph 774.
3. *Williams & Glyns* v. *Boland* [1981] AC 487.
4. *City of London Building Society* v. *Flegg* [1988] AC 54.
5. *Re Buchanan-Wollaston's Conveyance* [1939] Ch 738.
6. *Fairclough* v. *Swan Brewery Co. Ltd* [1912] AC565.
7. *Cuckmere Brick Co. Ltd* v. *Mutual Finance Ltd* [1971] Ch 949.
8. *London County Council* v. *Allen* [1914] 3KB 642.
9. *Elliston* v. *Reacher* [1908] 2 Ch 374.
10. *Re Ballards Conveyance* [1937] Ch 473.
11. *Re Ellenborough Park* [1956] Ch 473.
12. *Wheeldon* v. *Burrows* (1879) 12 ChD 131.
13. *Copeland* v. *Greenhalf* [1952] Ch 488.
14. *Wong* v. *Beaumont Property Trust Ltd* [1965] 1 QB 173.
15. *Boosey* v. *Davis* (1988) 55 P & CR 83.
16. *Morrice* v. *Evans, The Times* Feb 27 (1989) CA.

FURTHER READING

Böcker, M., Marzheuser, B., Nusser, M. and Scheja, K. (1992) *Germany: Practical Commercial Law*, Longman.

Cairns, W. and McKeon, R. (1995) *Introduction to French Law*, Cavendish.

Chappelle, D. (1995) *Land Law*, 2nd edn, Pitman.

Gray, K. (1993) *Elements of Land Law*, 2nd edn, Butterworths.

Riddall, J.G. (1993) *Introduction to Land* Law, 5th edn, Butterworths.

CHAPTER TEN

THE USE AND DEVELOPMENT OF LAND

LAURIE GRIMMETT, JEAN BADMAN AND PETER BARRETT

THEME

This chapter examines controls over the use of land and buildings under statutory law rather than the common law. Whilst not an exhaustive examination of this wide topic, certain statutes which are of importance to professionals working in this field are considered and will provide the basis on which to build more specialized examination of this branch of law.

OBJECTIVES

After reading this chapter you should be able to:

● understand the statutory basis of land use control;

● appreciate the need for the statutes which control land use;

● have a more in-depth knowledge of planning and development law and the reasons why this law affects all of the built environment professionals.

INTRODUCTION

The various stages through which parliamentary bills pass before they receive the Royal Assent have been discussed in Chapter 2. There are numerous Acts which control the way an owner develops, builds and uses land (and to a lawyer, the term 'land' includes buildings). For example, the Occupiers' Liability Acts impose liability to prevent harm occurring to visitors to a property; the Building Act relates to standards of construction of buildings; the Health and Safety at Work Act imposes duties on employers in connection with the safe use of their premises by their employees.

Most tenants of property have security of tenure. Essentially this is the right to occupy the premises with the knowledge that they will be entitled to a new lease at the end of the term of occupation granted by the lease, provided that they do not breach the tenancy agreement with their landlord.

For residential tenants whose tenancy commenced before 15 January 1989 protection is provided under the Rent Act 1977. In such cases at the end of the agreed term of occupation the landlord will only be able to recover vacant possession from the tenant by court order. The court will grant such an order only if the landlord can establish the following grounds:

- The tenant is in breach of covenant.
- The landlord can provide suitable alternative accommodation.
- The tenant is guilty of causing a nuisance or annoyance to neighbouring occupiers.

Certain lettings are excluded from this protection, including:

- holiday lettings;
- lettings to students where the landlord is the institution providing the students' course;
- lettings where the dwelling is part of a building which is partly used for business purposes;
- lettings where essential living rooms are shared;
- lettings where there is a resident landlord.

Since 15 January 1989 private sector housing and housing association tenants who have taken taken over residential tenancies are protected by the Housing Act 1988. The grounds for possession are similar to those under the Rent Act, with the addition that landlords can also obtain possession where they can establish a genuine intention to redevelop the site at the end of the lease.

Business tenants have protection under the Landlord and Tenant Act 1954. As with residential tenancies, if the tenant refuses to give up possession at the end of the lease the landlord who requires possession must obtain a court order. The grounds for possession are covered by Section 30 of the Act.

STATUTORY PROTECTION FOR OCCUPIERS OF PROPERTY BELONGING TO ANOTHER

OCCUPIERS' LIABILITY

Under the provisions of the Occupiers' Liability Act 1957 the occupier of land has a duty to ensure the safety of any person who is lawfully entitled to be on those premises. The duty is to ensure that as far as is reasonably possible the lawful entrant will not suffer injury or loss as a result of the dangerous condition of the premises or any part thereof. Premises include land, buildings or temporary structures, including, for example, scaffolding on a building site or a circus ring. It also includes movable objects such as ships, vehicles or aircraft [1].

The occupier is anyone who has a 'sufficient degree of control over the premises that he ought to realize that any failure on his part to use care may result in injury to a person lawfully coming there' [2]. This would include an owner-occupier in physical occupation of the premises but not necessarily an owner who has parted with possession in favour of a tenant. In such cases it will usually be the tenant who is the occupier for the purposes of the Act. In circumstances where landlords have retained overall control over the use and occupation of the property to the extent that they have some control over who may lawfully enter the premises, both the landlord and the tenant would be the occupier for the purposes of the Act and would share responsibility and liability (*Wheat* v. *Lacon* [1966] AC 552). Occupation therefore equals control. However, landlords who have not retained any control over the property may still be liable for loss or injury under the provisions of the Defective Premises Act 1972.

An occupier will not be liable for the negligent act or omission of an independent contractor responsible for the maintenance, repair or servicing of the property. In *Haseldine* v. *C.A. Daw and Son Ltd* [1941] 2KB 343 the occupiers of the building were not liable for the plaintiff's injuries caused by the negligence of an independent company engaged to service and maintain the lifts. Occupiers are, however, under a duty to demonstrate in such circumstances that they have taken reasonable care in appointing a competent contractor.

The occupier is liable only for injury suffered while the plaintiff is using the premises for the purpose for which he or she is lawfully permitted to be there [3]. Plaintiffs who make unauthorized use of the premises, or stray into an area where they are not permitted to have access, will be deemed to be trespassers and will not be covered by the Act [4]. Occupiers are, however, expected to realize that children often put themselves in the position of a trespasser without conscious realization of the implications. In such circumstances the occupier will owe a duty of common humanity and will be liable for any injury suffered by a child tresspasser in circumstances where the occupier realized or ought to have realized that there would be children on the premises and that due to the condition of the premises the child might be exposed to harm [5]. The standard of care owed is no higher than that of a reasonable parent or guardian [6].

The Occupiers' Liability Act 1984 has extended the occupier's liability to all trespassers in all circumstances where the occupier ought reasonably to have realized that trespassers could gain access to the premises and that the condition of the premises was such that they were dangerous.

Occupiers can discharge their duty by use of a warning to the entrant but any warning given must be such that in all the circumstances the entrant is made reasonably safe [7]. It is not enough merely to tell the entrant that the premises are not safe. The occupier must explain how the entrant can avoid injury. At common law no duty is owed to an entrant who knowingly accepts the risk of injury or harm. The entrant is expected to use the premises in a responsible way. Failure to do so may result in any damages awarded as a result of the occupier's liability under the Act being apportioned according to the provisions of the Law Reform (Contributory Negligence) Act 1945.

In addition to Acts of Parliament, controls are exercised through what is known as delegated legislation, through legal provisions made under the authority of Parliament by government departments.

There are a large number of statutes and delegated legislation controlling land concern issues which may not be of direct relevance to your own particular discipline within the built environment. Health and safety legislation, for example, and also the Occupiers' Liability Acts, will be particularly relevant to estate managers; the Building Act and legislation delegated under its powers will be of particular concern to architects or building surveyors.

WORKPIECE 10.1

OCCUPIERS' LIABILITY

Liability under the Occupiers' Liability Act 1957 depends primarily on occupation. Occupation, however, does not necessarily mean physical occupation in the usually accepted meaning of the word. Consider in what cirumstances a person who does not physically occupy premises may nevertheless be liable for the condition under the legislation.

However, whatever your discipline within this broad field of study, you will all be united in your need to understand the controls over the use and development of land imposed through planning legislation and its interpretation by the courts: the architect constrained to reduce the number of storeys in an imposing office building design from 20 floors to 12 as a result of a local planning authority's height restrictions in that locality; the builder erecting a village community hall, as a result of an agreement to allow an out-of-town retail development in return for providing local community facilities; the quantity surveyor hurriedly taking off altered quantities as a result of the alteration of the materials used for the façade of a proposed building, as a result of a planning condition; the estate manager whose valuation of a property is altered by refusal to allow a proposed, potentially valuable change of use of a building; the landscape architect designing the layout of a tree-planted area to screen a factory from a neighbouring residential area – the list is endless, and arises as a result of the application of planning legislation to your work in practice. Also, while you are a student carrying out joint project work with students of other disciplines within the built environment, you and all of your colleagues will be affected by the constraints of planning and development law.

Hence, although this chapter is of general relevance, the examples emphasize those statutes and associated delegated legislation which affect the use and development of land. It does not attempt to provide an all-embracing account of the sometimes complex provisions and of their interpretation by the judiciary, but it examines in detail aspects that, it is hoped, will be of interest to you and stimulate enthusiasm to delve more deeply into the texts and case law to which you will be referred.

PLANNING LEGISLATION

Planning legislation developed during the years after World War II, and was frequently amended. The legislation was consolidated in the Town and Country Planning Act 1990 and the Planning (Listed Buildings and Conservation Areas) Act 1990. Subsequent amendments to these Acts were made by the Planning and Compensation Act 1991.

TOWN AND COUNTRY PLANNING ACT 1990

This Act provides the powers for planning authorities to control the development and use of land within their areas of administration. The authorities with which you will deal in practice include local planning authorities (county and district councils), joint planning committees for Greater London, National Park Authorities, the Broads' Authority, enterprise zones, urban development corporations and housing action trusts.

Parish councils (community councils in Wales) have no planning powers, but they provide a particularly effective vehicle to promote local views. They are normally consulted on all planning applications within their respective areas, and can provide a considerable headache for would-be developers if they do not agree with any development proposal.

Whilst much of the administration and implementation of planning law is delegated to local authorities, considerable control is exercised by central government, and it is the Secretary of State for the Environment who has the overall responsibility for town and country planning.

DEVELOPMENT PLANS

The use and development of land is largely influenced by the production of 'development plans' and the implementation of a system of development control. No national plan exists to guide or influence development in the UK as a whole, but the Town and Country Planning Act 1990 imposes a duty on certain planning authorities to produce development plans for their area. England and Wales have moved towards a plan system which exists in many other European countries but it does have greater flexibility, allowing response to change, and hence is not merely an administrative process.

The existing system has two tiers of plan: the top tier, referred to as the **structure plan**, and the bottom tier, known as the **local plan**. These collectively comprise the development plan for most local planning authorities. In the old metropolitan county areas, **unitary development plans** (Parts I and II) are equivalent to structure and local plans.

STRUCTURE PLANS

These are normally produced by county planning authorities and provide a general strategic overview of policy for the county area. They comprise a written statement, key diagrams and other diagrammatic illustrations as are considered necessary. A written memorandum providing justification for the planning proposals, but not being a formal part of the plan itself, is also provided.

The form and content of structure plans is controlled through the Town and Country Planning Act 1990, as amended by the Planning and Compensation Act 1991 and by the Town and Country Planning (Development Plan) Regulations 1994, while government policy on their production and content is laid down by Planning Policy Guidance Note 12.

LOCAL PLANS

These provide more detail than structure plans, and hence they will have greater relevance to individual development control decisions. They consist of written policies supported by specific land use allocations (unlike structure plans, they utilize an Ordnance Survey map as their base). The Planning and Compensation Act 1991 requires all district planning authorities to produce a local plan covering the whole of their area, and this requirement extends to National Park authorities. Also, county planning authorities must produce a **local minerals plan** and a **waste local plan**.

The statutory development plans, both structure and local, must be taken into account when a planning authority considers any request for planning permission. The 1990 Act provides that:

> where, in making any determination under the planning Acts, regard is to be had to the development plan, the determination shall be made in accordance with the development plan unless material considerations indicate otherwise.

It is relevant to note, in the context of development plans, that it is not uncommon to find other documents in various forms that may have been produced by local planning authorities, but which have not necessarily gone through the statutory procedures required of development plans (particularly those requiring public participation in the making of the plans and their confirmation by the Secretary of State).

Whilst some of these informal documents will tend to disappear now that local plans have become mandatory, some (for example, design briefs and technical guidelines) will remain. As long as the nature of such documentation relates to the character of the use of land, they will be legally relevant documents and will be considered as one of the 'material considerations' in determining a planning application. They are, however, unlikely to have the same weight attached to them as the statutory development plan.

In concluding this examination of the structure and local plan requirements of the legislation, it is important to realize that development plans are permissive: they provide the backcloth against which planning decisions are taken, but they do not imply that planning permission will necessarily be given in a particular case.

In France, Germany and the Netherlands the local plan and building regulations are legally binding. A single permit will cover the control of development and control of building construction. In France, the local plan (*Plan d'Occupation des Sols*) is based on a zoning system and provides a statement of planning restrictions and opportunities; special protected zones may be designated. The zoning system is very inflexible and reflects British planning between the two World Wars.

PLANNING DOCUMENTS AND PLANS

Find out the current documents that are being used to control the use and development of land in an area with which you are familiar.

An application to the local planning authority is required when 'development' is to be carried out. The 1990 Act defines **development** as the carrying out of 'building, engineering, mining or other operations in, on, over or under land', and also making 'any material change of use'. This all-embracing definition means, if it were to be strictly applied, that even digging holes in the ground for the erection of fence posts requires planning permission from the local planning authority. To avoid planners being flooded with trivial applications of this kind, and to enable developers to operate with at least some degree of freedom, there are various exceptions to the requirement of obtaining formal permission.

WHEN IS PLANNING PERMISSION REQUIRED?

The legislation provides powers for the Secretary of State to prepare a list of categories of use, known as the Use Classes Order. This statutory instrument identifies 15 different categories of various uses. The significance of the Order is that provided that a change of use occurs within the same broad use class, it is not taken to involve the development of land and hence planning permission is not required. Thus, for example, a change from a greengrocer's shop to a hairdressing salon (both of which are in the A.1 Shop Use Class) would not require planning permission. Neither would the change of use of a building from a cinema to a snooker hall, as both are in the D2 Assembly and Leisure Class.

THE USE CLASSES ORDER 1987 (AS AMENDED)

The Town and Country Planning General Development Order 1988 was revoked with effect from 3 June 1995. Two new orders were introduced: one covers the procedure relating to planning applications now incorporated in the Town and Country Planning (General Development Procedure) Order 1995; the other is the Town and Country Planning (General Permitted Development) Order 1995, which grants specified permitted development rights.

The General Permitted Development Order (GPD) identifies a number of classes of permitted development. The effect of the Order is to grant permission for these development activities provided that they fall within the tolerances stated in the Order. The permitted classes, in

GENERAL DEVELOPMENT ORDERS (GDOs)

contrast to changes within the same use class, do in fact involve development but the GPD provides a blanket grant of permission, without the need to bother the local planning authority with a specific planning application. Note, however, that Building Regulations approval for any works which may be involved, and also any other necessary approvals such as entertainments or alcoholic drinks licences, will still be necessary.

At the time of writing, 33 categories of permitted development exist. These include Part One (development within the curtilage of a dwelling house) which will allow small extensions to residential property, subject to constraints on area, height, volume and proximity to neighbouring property and to the highway. It will also allow the erection of a satellite television dish on the outside wall of your house, again subject to certain constraints. Part Two (minor operations) permits operations in relation to gates, fences, walls and other means of enclosure and access; it also permits exterior painting. Hence, without the GPD everyone would be required to obtain planning permission before they could repaint the outside of their house!

It is worth noting that the GPD also includes provision for the withdrawal of permitted development rights under GPD4. Also, the GPD has a link with the Use Classes Order, in that certain changes of use (although not within the same use class) are identified in the GPD as permitted – for example, change from an A3 use (food and drink) to an A1 use (shops).

CONDITIONAL PLANNING PERMISSION

Local planning authorities have statutory power to attach conditions to the grant of planning permissions, and more often than not they exercise their power. The building must be no more than two storeys, the night club must close before midnight, the perimeter of the factory site must be screened with trees – a plethora of restrictions on the development and subsequent use of the site and the proposed building may be imposed. Conditions may well affect your design, your estimated development costs and, of particular concern to the owner, the market value of the completed development.

The power to impose conditions is, prima facie, very wide – planning authorities may impose such conditions 'as they think fit'. This phrase first appeared in the Town and Country Planning Act 1947, and was included in the legislation by a Labour government facing enormous post-war planning and reconstruction of large parts of cities and towns damaged by bombing and by lack of maintenance during the war years. Planners were to be left to plan, free from interference. However, over the years the courts have curbed that apparently wide power.

Conditions may be challenged by the aggrieved applicant, by appeal to the Secretary of State and thence, if that appeal is unsuccessful, to the High Court. It will be recalled from Chapter 2 that a judge interpreting a statute frequently takes the literal meaning of the words of the Act. Often, however, it is the intention of Parliament when it passed the Act which is considered. In deciding on the validity of planning conditions, the judiciary has frequently taken the stance that particular conditions are so unreasonable that Parliament could surely not have intended that the power should be so wide. In *Pyx Granite Co. Ltd* v. *Ministry of Housing and Local Government* [1960] AC260, Lord Denning MR held that conditions must fairly and reasonably relate to the proposed development, and that the planning authority may not impose conditions for an ulterior object. Thus, in deciding whether a challenge to a planning condition is likely to be successful, the test of Lord Denning in the Pyx Granite case is applied – if the condition fails that test, it is ultra vires (beyond the statutory powers), but if it satisfies that test, it is within the planning authority's powers (intra vires).

Lord Denning's view of a valid planning condition was approved by the House of Lords in *Fawcett Properties Ltd* v. *Buckingham County Council* [1961] AC636. The condition in dispute required cottages to be occupied only by agricultural workers. As such a condition restricts value, particularly in areas within commuting reach of urban areas, the company challenged the condition on the grounds that it was beyond the powers of the planning authority – planners may tell an owner how properties are to be used (here, for residential purposes), but not who is to occupy them. This ultra vires claim was not accepted by their Lordships: the aim of the condition was to preserve a rural environment and part of the local authority's planning policy, and that was a perfectly valid policy. You may query how commuters living in what were in fact only two cottages in the Green Belt could have threatened the rural environment, but local planning authorities frequently refuse planning applications, or attach onerous conditions, when they are concerned that they may be setting a precedent, making it difficult to justify refusal of similar applications from other owners.

Contrast this approval of a planning condition by the courts with the decision in *R.* v. *Hillingdon London Borough Council*, ex parte *Royco Homes Ltd* [1974] QB 720. Here, in granting planning permission for residential development, the local planning authority had attached conditions requiring the houses to be built to the space and cost standards normally required of council housing; also, the houses were to be let rather than sold, the rents were to be controlled, and the tenants were to be selected from the council house waiting list. The court held that the conditions were clearly ultra vires, as the authority was attempting to pass on its statutory housing duties to a private developer.

The decision in this case is in sharp contrast with that of *Fawcett Properties Ltd* v. *Buckingham County Council*. In Fawcett, the condition was used for a social purpose – to ensure the houses, in a rural area, would be available for occupation by local agricultural workers, and such conditions were within the authority's statutory powers. In the Hillingdon case, the local authority, with insufficient funds to build enough council houses to satisfy the demand within the borough, was also attempting to apply conditions for a similar social purpose, but this was declared ultra vires. Judicial views of the validity of conditions are not always consistent. For an interesting discussion on this point, see Patrick McAuslan's comments in *Ideologies of Planning Law*.

Another case illustrating ultra vires conditions, and their effect on planning permission, is *Hall & Co. Ltd* v. *Shoreham-by-Sea Urban District Council* [1964] 1 All ER1. Permission for industrial development was subject to conditions requiring the company to build a road along the frontage of its site, at the company's expense, and to allow neighbouring property owners and their visitors to use the road. It was held that such conditions were clearly ultra vires – they were in effect requiring a private developer to carry out the council's statutory highway duties at their own expense. However, the court refused to strike out the offending conditions, leaving the permission in force to enable the company to carry on with its proposed development. In reaching this decision, the court relied on Lord Denning's views in the Pyx Granite case, where he had held that if a fundamental condition is declared invalid by the courts, then the whole permission is void. Lord Denning's justification for this was that if the local planning authority had not had the opportunity to impose particular conditions when granting planning permission, it might not have granted permission at all.

This is a correct interpretation of the planning application process. For example, in considering an application for change of use of a building to a fish and chip shop in a residential area, a planning authority might have doubts concerning the effects of the new use on the amenity of local residents. It might feel, however, that those doubts will be allayed by imposing a condition that the shop must close at 11 p.m. each night, but if it were denied the opportunity to impose that condition, it might not have granted permission for the change of use. One of the objects of good planning is to separate incompatible uses, or to minimize any detrimental effects of one development on neighbouring developments and their users.

Lord Denning's clinching argument in Pyx Granite was that it is not the work of judges to write planning conditions – that is the function of planners, and of the Secretary of State on appeal, as head of the modus operandi of planning legislation: judges are judges, not planners. A developer might, on the basis of these decisions, therefore be wasting time in challenging a condition beyond appeal to the Secretary of State, as there is a risk that the permission will be lost entirely. However, the 1990 Act provides assistance.

WORKPIECE 10.3

PLANNING CONDITIONS

Visit your local planning department and examine the register of planning decisions. Make a list of five different planning conditions that have been attached to planning approvals during recent weeks.

SECTION 73 APPEAL PROCEDURE

This section of the 1990 legislation overcomes the problem of losing the whole permission if the court strikes out a condition on ultra vires grounds. It involves, first, making an application to the local planning authority which has granted permission with conditions, requesting that the conditions be ignored. The authority must then consider the conditions in isolation, and it may, if it wishes, grant unconditional permission. As the authority may only recently have granted the original permission, it is hardly likely to remove the conditions, but it may do so. If it does not, there is then a right of appeal to the Secretary of State, and if the latter refuses to lift the conditions, appeal then lies to the High court, on a point of law. The court is then required to examine the legality of the conditions, considered in isolation from the permission, and if the court is satisfied that the condition is ultra vires it will be removed, however fundamental it is to the whole permission, but leaving the permission itself intact. This procedure has not yet been tested in the courts and it remains to be seen how the judiciary will interpret this section in the light of Lord Denning's stricture that judges consider matters of law – they cannot comment on the merits of planning permissions with or without conditions. Certainly, this procedure will exercise legal minds in future.

PLANNING (LISTED BUILDINGS AND CONSERVATION AREAS) ACT 1990

The statutory provisions relating to buildings of architectural merit or historical interest were previously incorporated in town and country planning legislation, but in 1990 the protection afforded such buildings (and also conservation areas) was consolidated and amended in separate legislation, the Planning (Listed Buildings and Conservation Areas) Act 1990.

The Secretary of State for National Heritage, after consultation with English Heritage and various pressure groups, such as the Victorian Society, approves lists of buildings considered to be of architectural or historical merit. The buildings are graded as Grade I (buildings of exceptional interest), Grade II* (particularly important, but not of outstanding grade) and Grade II (of special interest, but not of the quality of the other two grades). The lists of these buildings may be inspected at local planning authority offices, and the significance to you in advising clients is that any works which will alter the character of a listed building requires 'listed building consent', in addition to planning permission for any works of development. This involves an application to the local planning authority, and there is a right of appeal if consent is refused – to the Secretary of State and thence the courts. It should be noted that listed building consent may therefore be required for works which are not 'development' within the meaning of the Town and Country Planning Act 1990, or which are types of development that do not require a specific planning application (the 'deemed consent' provisions of the current General Permitted Development Order 1995). For example, even changing the colour of external woodwork, or rendering the brickwork of external walls, may, in the opinion of the local planning authority, change the character of the building. The ultimate change of character is, of course, the unauthorized demolition of a listed building.

PENALTIES

It is an offence to carry out such works to a listed building without having first obtained listed building consent. The Planning and Compensation Act 1991 has raised the maximum fine which may be imposed in the magistrates' courts to £20 000; alternatively, a maximum sentence of two years' imprisonment may be the penalty if the case is considered serious enough to justify indictment before the Crown Court, where the fine level is unlimited.

It is acknowledged that the imposition of fines, particularly at magistrate level, may be a relatively trivial deterrent to the developer, but the risk of a term in prison does far more to concentrate the mind of the developer considering the unlawful demolition of a building. Although prison sentences have been relatively rare in this field, the courts may well now be more likely to impose custodial sentences. In the West Country, for example, a builder who had obtained listed building consent to convert a listed chapel building into flats, with a condition that he retained the original façade, was tempted to use a small explosive charge to cause a structural crack in the building, thus making it dangerous. This, he assumed, would lead to consent for demolition from the local authority. Unfortunately, the amount of explosive was over-estimated and the charge demolished the building. The builder was imprisoned and the publicity attached to a case of this kind does far more than fines to dissuade builders and developers from carrying out works without the necessary consent.

In addition, local planning authorities have made use of another and effective means of punishment, by making the offender rebuild.

LISTED BUILDING ENFORCEMENT NOTICES

Local planning authorities can make use of the listed building enforcement notice procedure, whereby the developer is served notice to reinstate the now felled building brick by brick, or stone by stone. If the demolished materials have been removed from the site, the enforcement notice may even chase the parts. In *R. v. Leominster District Council*, ex parte *Antique Country Buildings Ltd* [1988] JPL 554, a listed barn had been dismantled and packed, ready to be shipped to the USA. The owners were required to bring the parts back to the original site and rebuild.

The likelihood that this action will be taken, resulting in considerable costs of rebuilding, is an even more effective deterrent than a £20 000 fine which might be imposed on summary conviction.

DEMOLITION USING THE LAW

Although the protective provisions of the legislation might well be criticized as being of little consequence to an unscrupulous developer, there is in fact a considerable amount of protection and deterrence against unauthorized demolition.

However, there are circumstances where it might be possible to obtain the approval of the courts. The first chink in the growing protection of heritage buildings occurred in *R. v. Westminster City Council*, ex parte *Monahan* (the Royal Opera House case) [1988] JPL 107, where the court refused to intervene in the proposed demolition of listed buildings near the Opera House. The site was to be redeveloped with commercial buildings, the income from which would be used to finance the Opera House, and it was held that such financial considerations were material in deciding whether to allow consent to demolish, and that these considerations took precedence over the architectural merit of the existing buildings.

173

This thin wedge inserted into the policy of preserving heritage buildings was hammered home more firmly in 1991, by the decision in *SAVE Britain's Heritage* v. *No.1 Poultry Ltd* [1991] 2 All ER 10. The dispute concerned a challenge made by a historic buildings pressure group against the Secretary of State's decision to grant listed building consent for the demolition of eight listed buildings at No.1 Poultry Ltd (the 'Mappin and Webb site'), together with a number of other buildings not listed, but within a Conservation Area.

The owner proposed to construct a single modern building providing 240 000 square feet (22 300 m²) of office and retail accommodation in the heart of the City. The architectural proposals had a somewhat drawn-out genesis. An earlier proposal had been made to develop this and a nearby site with a scheme designed by the late Mies van der Rohe. This application had been rejected by the local planning authority and by the Secretary of State on appeal. The Secretary's decision was that the Mies van der Rohe building would dominate the site and its surroundings unacceptably and there would be stark contrast between the proposed building and the scale and character of neighbouring buildings. However, in that decision, in 1985, the Secretary did not rule out the possibility of redevelopment if there were proposals to replace the existing buildings with acceptable substitutes, as he considered it would be wrong to freeze the character of the City for all time. Thus the way was made open for the owner to suggest a more modest proposal, albeit offering 240 000 sq. ft of modern floor space.

James Stirling, later Sir James, was appointed to design the substituted proposal. The new scheme was described by HRH Prince Charles as looking like a '1930s wireless set', but attracted praise from the architectural profession. A new application for listed building and conservation area consent to demolish the building and the application for planning permission for the scheme were rejected by the local planning authority, but allowed by the Secretary of State on appeal. Save Britain's Heritage pursued what they saw as an important principle, which if allowed to stand would threaten more heritage buildings. Save claimed that the Secretary of State had given inadequate reasons for his decision, which was contrary to his own policy guidelines on listed buildings. Those guidelines, which were contained in Circular 8/87, included a presumption in favour of retaining listed buildings, rather than allowing them to be demolished, unless it could be shown that a particular building under consideration could not be economically retained, for example by a refurbishment scheme. Save produced such a scheme, and all the

174

parties involved in the dispute agreed that the scheme was viable and would enable the existing buildings to be retained. Nevertheless, the Secretary had granted consent for demolition.

The Secretary of State's reason for not following his own Circular 8/87 policy was that the proposed replacement buildings would be of greater architectural merit than the existing buildings. The House of Lords held that the Secretary was entitled to make an exception to his own guidelines, and the reason given was adequate. It should be noted that the courts cannot comment on matters of architecture – judges are neither architects nor planners. The fact that everyone else may do so, from Prince Charles downwards, is neither here nor there. In reaching his decision, the Secretary of State had taken advice from one of his inspectors, in this case an architect.

The consequences of this decision may well cause future concern to groups promoting the protection of listed buildings. The developer's ideal for, say, an office block is one of large, open-space floors which give a maximum return in rent levels and consequently in capital value. Listed buildings occupying valuable sites in city centres all too often have thick internal walls, large open staircases and too much wasted corridor space, and they require expensive, regular maintenance. The site, if only consent to demolish could be obtained, is the attraction to the property developer. All that will now be required is a proposed replacement of greater architectural merit. Sir James Stirling is regrettably now deceased, but there are plenty of architects who would be willing to fill the gap by using their design skills to accept the challenge of producing a design judged by architects, and the Secretary of State on appeal, as being of more merit than the Georgian office building it will replace. If consent to demolish is refused by the local planning authority, appeal can be made to the Secretary of State (and thence the courts if necessary), citing the Save Britain's Heritage decision, and down will come the building.

WORKPIECE 10.4

LISTED BUILDINGS

The law offers some protection against the unauthorized demolition of a listed building.

- What protection exists?
- What improvements, if any, to those measures do you suggest and why?

BUILDING PRESERVATION NOTICES

These are used to protect buildings which are not listed, but which a local planning authority considers should be listed. Although the lists are revised frequently, there are occasions where a rapid form of protection is needed – for example, if a civic society makes representations to the planning authority that a particular building has historical or architectural value which would justify listing, but the society points out that demolition equipment is being assembled on the site. In such instances the planning authority may serve on the owner a building preservation notice. This brings all the provisions of the Act to the building, even though it is not listed – the enforcement powers, the need for listed consent, the fines, etc. At the same time, service of the notice is coupled with a request by the local authority for the Secretary of State to list the building, and he has six months in which to do so. If the decision is not to list, a further preservation notice cannot be served by the local authority for a further 12 months, which gives the owner time to demolish and submit a planning application for development of the site.

At first sight, this seems to be a useful and effective means of protecting buildings which might, after careful consideration, be worthy of listing. However, the problem for the local planning authority is that if the Secretary of State decides not to list the building, compensation is payable, by the local planning authority, to the developer whose proposal has been frustrated for up to six months. This may involve considerable sums – for example, sale of the completed development has been delayed six months, and the £10 million realized on sale could have been invested elsewhere, earning interest; the building contractor has to relocate the workforce, machinery and materials, and may claim for breach of contract by the developer. Any such claim may be passed on to the planning authority in the compensation claim. Risks of this kind means that the planning authority must be wary, and confident in its reasoning, when attempting to obtain listed status for a building it thinks is in danger of being demolished.

ANCIENT MONUMENTS

Whilst it is apparent that controls over the development of sites containing listed buildings may frequently pose difficult questions for professional advisers, the law relating to the protection of ancient monuments may lead to equally thorny problems. The main legislation here is the Ancient Monuments and Archaeological Areas Act 1979, but there is some overlapping control exercised under the Town and Country Planning Act 1990.

The meaning of the term 'monument' is wider than that of 'listed building' in that the former includes not only buildings and other structures but also a bare site. Thus if a field is reputed to have been the site of even a preliminary skirmish of soldiers on their way to, say, a Civil War battle, the owner contemplating building an estate of expensive houses may find the scheme (and profits) delayed for several months, without compensation, while archaeologists painstakingly dig the soil in the hope of finding historically significant artefacts.

An 'ancient monument' is a monument which, in the opinion of the Secretary of State for National Heritage, is of historical or archaeological interest. It may or may not have architectural merit as well. The maximum protection afforded by the 1979 Act is given to monuments included by the Secretary of State in a schedule of ancient monuments considered to be of national importance. In addition to well-known monuments such as Stonehenge and the Tower of London, the schedule extends to thousands of less well-known structures, such as church ruins, stones and crosses.

It is an offence under the 1979 Act to carry out works to an ancient monument without first having obtained scheduled monument consent. Works are defined to include demolition, damage, alterations, repair – even flooding a site, or tipping waste debris on it, requires consent. If the Secretary considers that works are urgently needed to preserve a scheduled monument, the Department may enter and carry out the required remedial work but, unlike listed building legislation, it is unable to recover the costs from the owner.

The 1979 Act also contains provisions which allow the Secretary of State for National Heritage to designate sites which are considered to be of archaeological significance. These areas, while they may already include individual scheduled and unscheduled monuments, are given protection over the whole locality, as they may contain archaeological objects which might be revealed only by future excavation. Thus the purpose of designating these areas, which so far are the centres of historic towns (Canterbury, Hereford, York, Chester and Exeter), is to allow archaeologists time to excavate and record before development proposals are implemented. The developer may not disturb the ground without first having served an 'operations notice' on the local authority, at least six weeks before the development is due to commence. The local authority, or a university archaeological department to whom the authority delegates the work, may then excavate the site before development takes place, and may delay commencement of the proposed development for up to six months from the service of the operations notice.

UNSCHEDULED ANCIENT MONUMENTS

Although a greater degree of protection is given to scheduled monuments, and unscheduled monuments in areas of archaeological importance, there are limited protective powers for mere unscheduled monuments under the 1979 Act. For example, the Secretary of State has compulsory purchase powers to acquire all legal interests in any monument, whether scheduled or not, if this is necessary to ensure the maintenance of the monument; sometimes these interests are also acquired by agreement with the owners. If the owner is unable to maintain a monument (for example, on grounds of financial hardship), the Secretary of State may become the 'guardian' of the monument: the owner retains a legal interest in the monument, but the Secretary takes on the control, and costs, of care and maintenance.

ANCIENT MONUMENTS AND THE TOWN AND COUNTRY PLANNING ACT 1990

There are also protective provisions in the 1990 Act which add to the procedures of the 1979 Act. For example, the local planning authority, in deciding on a planning application, may take account of the effect of a proposed development on an ancient monument when it decides on the grant or refusal of planning permission; it may add conditions to the permission, perhaps involving preservation, protection or restoration of the monument. Such powers extend not merely to scheduled monuments: the authority might, say, call for archaeological excavation of an unscheduled monument before development commences, or require access for an archaeologist to observe while the development is carried out, to enable recording and examination of any artefacts of interest, and as a result an unscheduled monument may then be considered worthy of scheduling.

COMPENSATION

There is no compensation available to the owner of a site which is scheduled by the Secretary of State, nor where the site is an ancient monument which is not scheduled but which is subject to a planning condition delaying development until excavation has taken place. However, if planning permission for development is granted but the site later becomes scheduled (e.g. because of items of significance unearthed by the builder during site excavation works), and development is then prevented because of the scheduling, compensation for loss of development value is payable to the owner. In *R. v. Secretary of State for the Environment,* ex parte *Rose Theatre Trust Co.* [1990] 1 QB 504, the Secretary of State had refused to schedule the site of the former Rose Theatre, where some of Shakespeare's plays were first performed. The Secretary had refused to schedule on the grounds that compensation might be payable to the developers, and the High Court dismissed the application to quash his decision as the compensation risk was a relevant consideration for the Secretary to take into account. The developer's offer (which was in fact later implemented) to preserve the remains of the theatre and allow headroom beneath the development for future inspection was also a relevant factor in reaching the decision not to schedule the site.

Finally, you will have noticed during reading this discussion on ancient monuments legislation that there is far less detailed protection when compared with the law protecting listed buildings. There is also an overlap between the Ancient Monuments Act 1979 and the ancient monuments provisions in the Town and Country Planning Act 1990. There is a distinct impression that the 1979 Act required more thought by the legislators before being enacted, and it is disappointing that the opportunity was not taken, when the Listed Buildings Act 1990 was proceeding through Parliament, to consolidate ancient monuments legislation into the same Act, so that there could be one legislative code for these two important aspects of heritage law.

WORKPIECE 10.5

ANCIENT MONUMENTS AND DEVELOPMENT

A developer owns a field on the edge of a market town which is zoned in the local plan for residential use. Before the developer has applied for planning permission for residential development, however, the Secretary of State is advised that there is clear evidence that the field is the site of a former Viking settlement, and has consequently now scheduled the field as an ancient monument.

What are the likely effects of this on the developer's proposed scheme?

SUMMARY

The manner in which owners develop and use their land is restricted by the law, which often leads to disputes which require referral to the courts. In this respect of the law, planning legislation is particularly important to professionals working in the built environment as it affects all of them, directly or indirectly. This law is complex and it provides the prime example of why the study of law is essential to built environment students.

This chapter has:

● considered some of the legislation that controls the way an owner develops, builds or uses land (which includes buildings);

- examined the Town and Country Planning Act 1990 and its influence on land use and development;
- looked at some of the special controls on lands and property including the Planning (Listed Buildings and Conservation Areas) Act 1990 and the Ancient Monuments and Archaeological Areas Act 1979;
- examined the way in which law and policy has been interpreted by the courts.

CHECKLIST

- The relationship of landlords and tenants of residential property is controlled by the Rent Act 1977 and the Housing Acts.
- Tenants of business properties have protection under the Landlord and Tenant Acts.
- Visitors, as opposed to owners or occupiers, are owed a duty of safety and care under the Occupiers' Liability Acts.
- The development of land is controlled by local planning authorities under town and country planning legislation, under the overall control of the Secretary of State for the Environment.
- However, the Secretary of State for National Heritage is also influential in this field, as this Department is responsible for overseeing the protection which the law provides for listed buildings and ancient monuments.

REFERENCES

1. Occupiers' Liability Act 1957 section 1(3)(a).
2. Per Lord Denning *Wheat* v. *Lacon and Co. Ltd* [1966] AC 442.
3. *The Calgarth* [1927] P93.
4. *Westwood* v. *Post Office* [1973] 1 QB 591.
5. *British Railway Board* v. *Herrington* [1972] AC 877.
6. *Phipps* v. *Rochester Corp.* [1955] 1 QB 450.
7. Occupiers' Liability Act 1957 section 2(4)(a).

FURTHER READING

Asimov, M. (1983) *Delegated legislation. United States and United Kingdom*, Oxford University Press, Oxford.

Moore, V. (1995) *A Practical Approach to Planning Law*, 5th edn, Blackstone Press.

McAuslan, P. (1980) *The Ideologies of Planning Law*, Pergamon Press.

Telling, A.E. and Duxbury, R.M.C. (1993) *Planning Law and Procedure*, 9th edn, Butterworths.

INDEX

181